C. M. Barnes

Sweet Harmonies

a new song book of gospel songs for use in revivals and all religious gatherings, Sunday-schools, etc.

C. M. Barnes

Sweet Harmonies
a new song book of gospel songs for use in revivals and all religious gatherings, Sunday-schools, etc.

ISBN/EAN: 9783337265618

Printed in Europe, USA, Canada, Australia, Japan

Cover: Foto ©Lupo / pixelio.de

More available books at **www.hansebooks.com**

SWEET HARMONIES

A NEW SONG BOOK

—— OF ——

GOSPEL * SONGS

— FOR USE IN —

REVIVALS AND ALL RELIGIOUS GATHERINGS,
SUNDAY-SCHOOLS, ETC.

COMPOSED AND SELECTED

—— BY ——

C. M. BARNES.

Address all orders for books to C. M. Barnes, Eureka Springs, Ark.,

1896:
PUBLISHED BY
C. M. BARNES.

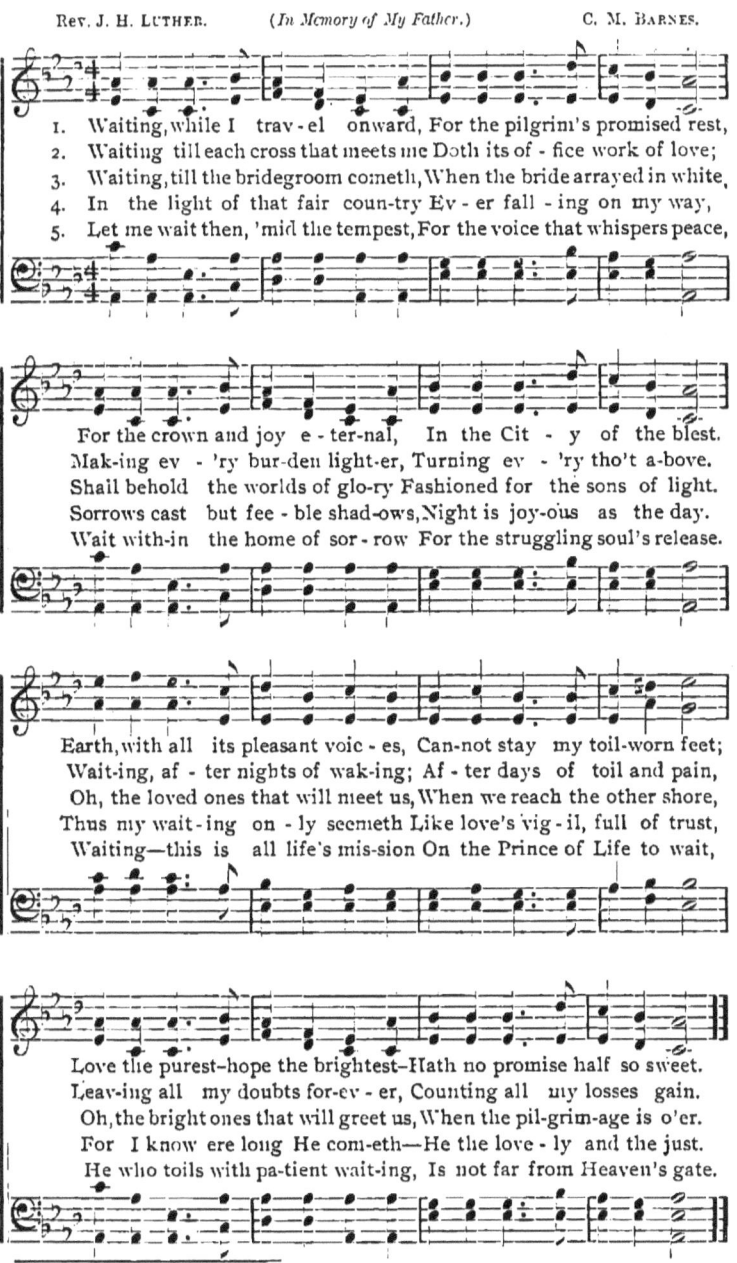

No. 4. Tell It Out, (Missionary.)

"The Lord is King forever and ever." Psa. 10:15.

FRANCES R. HAVERGAL. CHAS. EDW. POLLOCK. By per.

With Vigor.

1. Tell it out a-mong the na-tions That the Lord is King; Tell it out! Tell it out! Tell it out among the nations, bid them shout and sing; Tell it out! Tell it out! Tell it out! Tell it out! with ad-o-ra-tion that He shall increase, Tell it out! Tell it out! That the mighty King of glo-ry is the King of peace, Tell it out!

2. Tell it out a-mong the peo-ple That the Sav-ior reigns, Tell it out! Tell it out! Tell it out among the heathen, bid them break their chains; Tell it out! Tell it out! Tell it out! Tell it out! among the weeping ones that Je-sus lives, Tell it out! Tell it out! Tell it out a-mong the weary ones what rest He gives, Tell it out!

3. Tell it out a-mong the peo-ple, Je-sus reigns a-bove; Tell it out! Tell it out! Tell it out among the nations, That His reign is love; Tell it out! Tell it out! Tell it out! Tell it out! among the highways and the lanes at home, Tell it out! Tell it out! Let it ring across the mountains and the ocean's foam, Tell it out!

Tell It Out—Concluded.

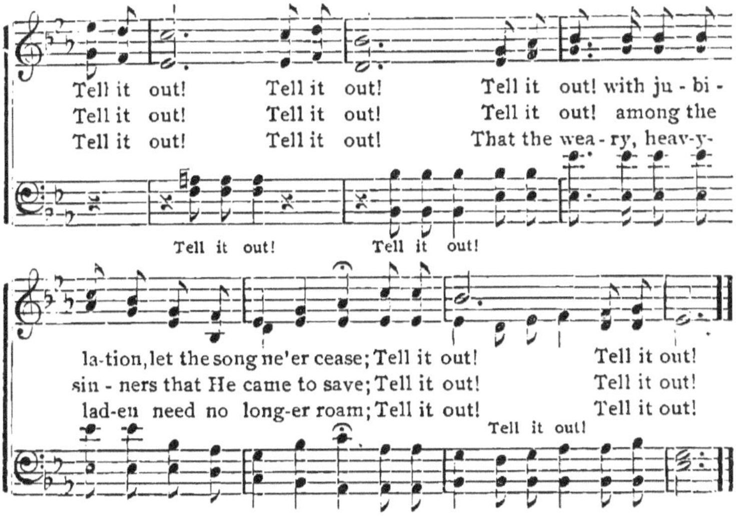

Tell it out! Tell it out! Tell it out! with ju-bi-
Tell it out! Tell it out! Tell it out! among the
Tell it out! Tell it out! That the wea-ry, heav-y-

Tell it out! Tell it out!

la-tion, let the song ne'er cease; Tell it out! Tell it out!
sin-ners that He came to save; Tell it out! Tell it out!
lad-en need no long-er roam; Tell it out! Tell it out!
Tell it out!

No. 5. Martyn, 7s, D.

S. B. Marsh. 1798-1834.
FINE.

1. { Je-sus, lov-er of my soul, Let me to Thy bo-som fly,
   { While the nearer wa-ters roll, While the tempest still is high;
D. C.—Safe in-to the ha-ven guide, O re-ceive my soul at last.

2. { Oth-er ref-uge have I none; Hangs my helpless soul on Thee;
   { Leave, ah! leave me not a-lone, Still support and comfort me!
D. C.—Cov-er my defenseless head With the shad-ow of Thy wing.

D. C.

Hide me, O my Sav-ior, hide, Till the storm of life is past;
All my trust on Thee is stayed, All my help from Thee I bring;

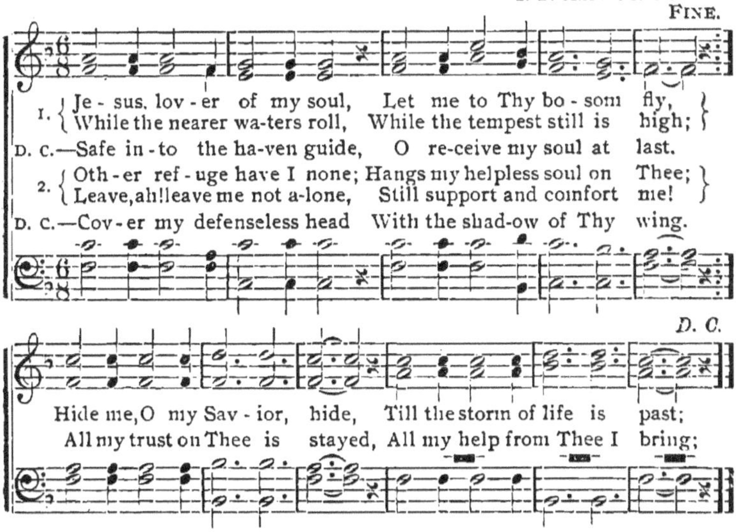

3 Thou, O Christ, art all I want;
  More than all in Thee I find;
  Raise the fallen, cheer the faint,
  Heal the sick, and lead the blind.
  Just and holy is thy name;
  I am all unrighteousness;
  Vile and full of sin I am,
  Thou art full of truth and grace.

4 Plenteous grace with Thee is found,
  Grace to cover all my sin;
  Let the healing stream abound,
  Make and keep me pure within.
  Thou of Life the Fountain art;
  Freely let me take of Thee;
  Spring thou up within my heart,
  Rise to all eternity.

By and By—Concluded.

by, Then we'll shout and sing together by and by.
by and by, by and by.

No. 13. How Firm a Foundation.

1. How firm a foun-da-tion, ye saints of the Lord, Is laid for your
2. In ev-'ry con-di-tion, in sick-ness, in health, In pov-er-ty's
3. E'en down to old age all my peo-ple shall prove My sov'reign, e-
4. The soul that on Je-sus hath leaned for re-pose, I will not, I

faith in His ex-cel-lent word! What more can He say than to
vale or a-bound-ing in wealth; At home and a-broad, on the
ter-nal, un-change-a-ble love; And when hoary hairs shall their
will not de-sert to its foes; That soul, tho' all hell should en-

you He hath said, You who un-to Je-sus for ref-uge have fled?
land, on the sea, As your days may demand shall your strength ever be,
tem-ples a-dorn, Like lambs they shall still in my bo-som be borne.
deav-or to shake, I'll nev-er, no, nev-er, no nev-er for-sake!

No. 14. Turned Away From the Beautiful Gate.

"Lord, Lord, open to us, But He shall say, I know you not, depart from me."
D. E. DORTCH.   Luke 13:25, 27.   D. E. DORTCH.

Not too fast.

1. Some one will knock at the saints' bright home, And hear the Lord saying, "You can-not come;" With sad-ness he'll mourn o'er his sor-row-ful state;
2. Some one will hear the angel's song, And wish he could join with the hap-py throng, With sigh-ing he'll mourn o'er his sor-row-ful state;
3. Some one will stand with an aching heart, While Je-sus pronounces the word, "depart;" With groan-ings he'll mourn o'er his sor-row-ful state;
4. Some one will lin-ger with tearful eyes, While Christ and His people as-cend the skies; With weeping he'll mourn o'er his sor-row-ful state;
5. Some one will go in-to darkness drear, Far off from the Sav-ior and all that's dear; With anguish he'll mourn o'er his sor-row-ful state;
6. Some one will en-ter the door of hell, And hear the sad wailings no tongue can tell; With hor-ror he'll mourn o'er his sor-row-ful state;

REFRAIN.

Turned a-way from the beautiful gate, Turned away from the beau-ti-ful gate, Turned a-way from the beau-ti-ful gate; With sadness he'll mourn o'er his sorrowful state, Turned away from the beau-ti-ful gate.

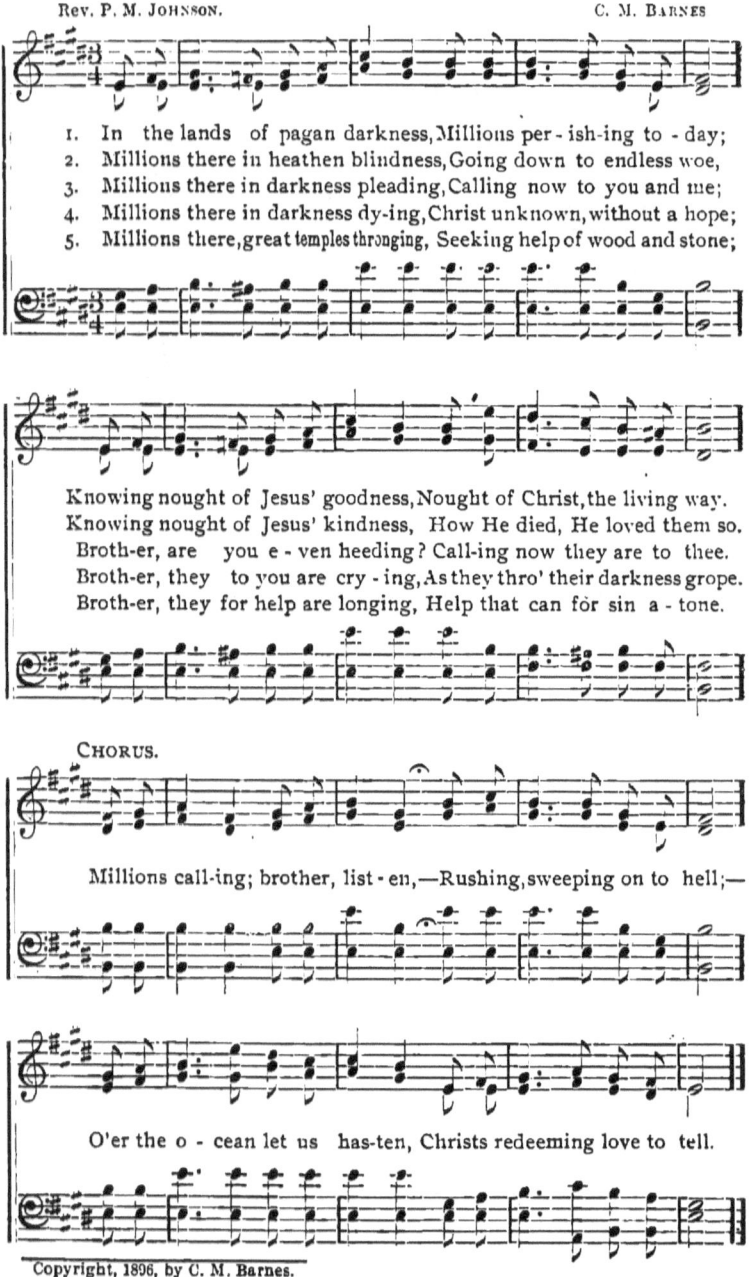

No. 17. Tell Me All About Jesus.

Rev. Elisha A. Hoffman. Chas. Edw. Pollock. By per.

1. Tell me all about Jesus, Who came from heav'n above;
2. Tell me all about Jesus, The Lamb of Calvary;
3. Tell me all about Jesus, Who daily cares for me;
4. Tell me all about Jesus, Repeat the story o'er;

Tell me more of His goodness, More of His precious love.
Tell me more of His mercy, More of His grace to me.
Tell me why He should love me, Why He should die for me.
Never shall I grow weary, Hearing it more and more.

CHORUS.

Tell me all about Jesus, Tell me that I may know
The story of the Savior Who loves, who loves me so.

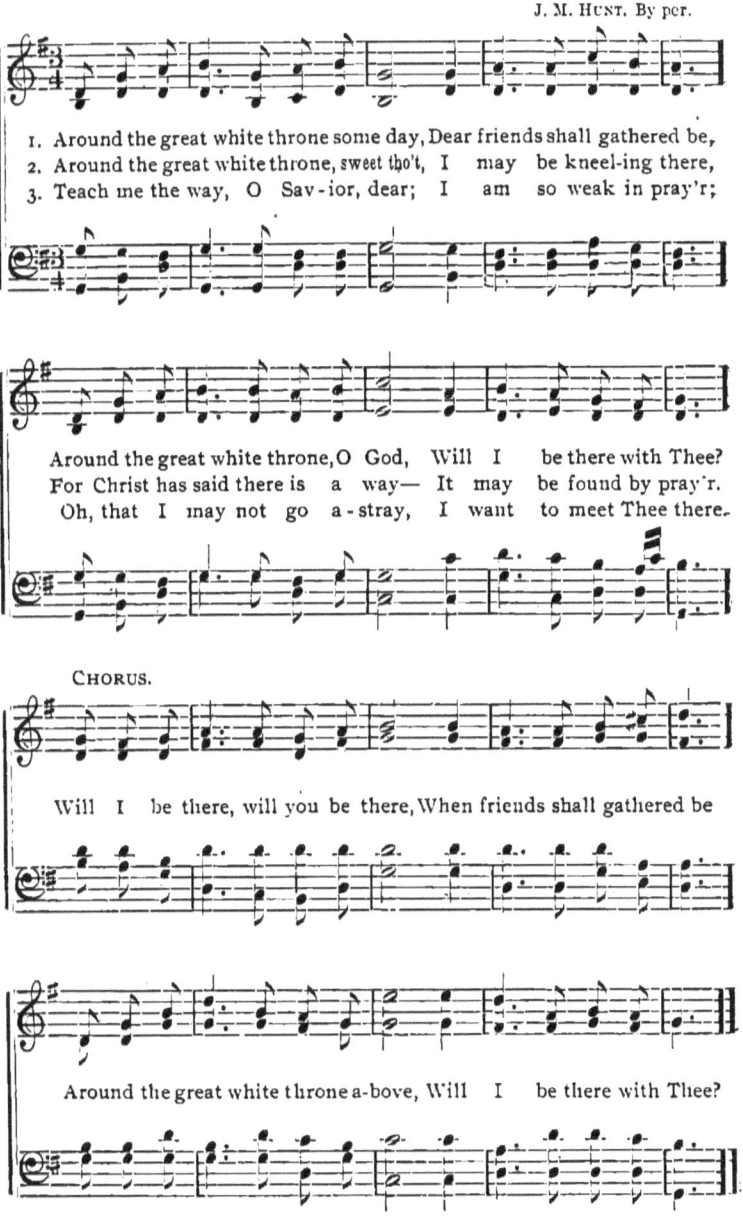

No. 20. Hear the Message.

C. M. B.   C. M. Barnes.

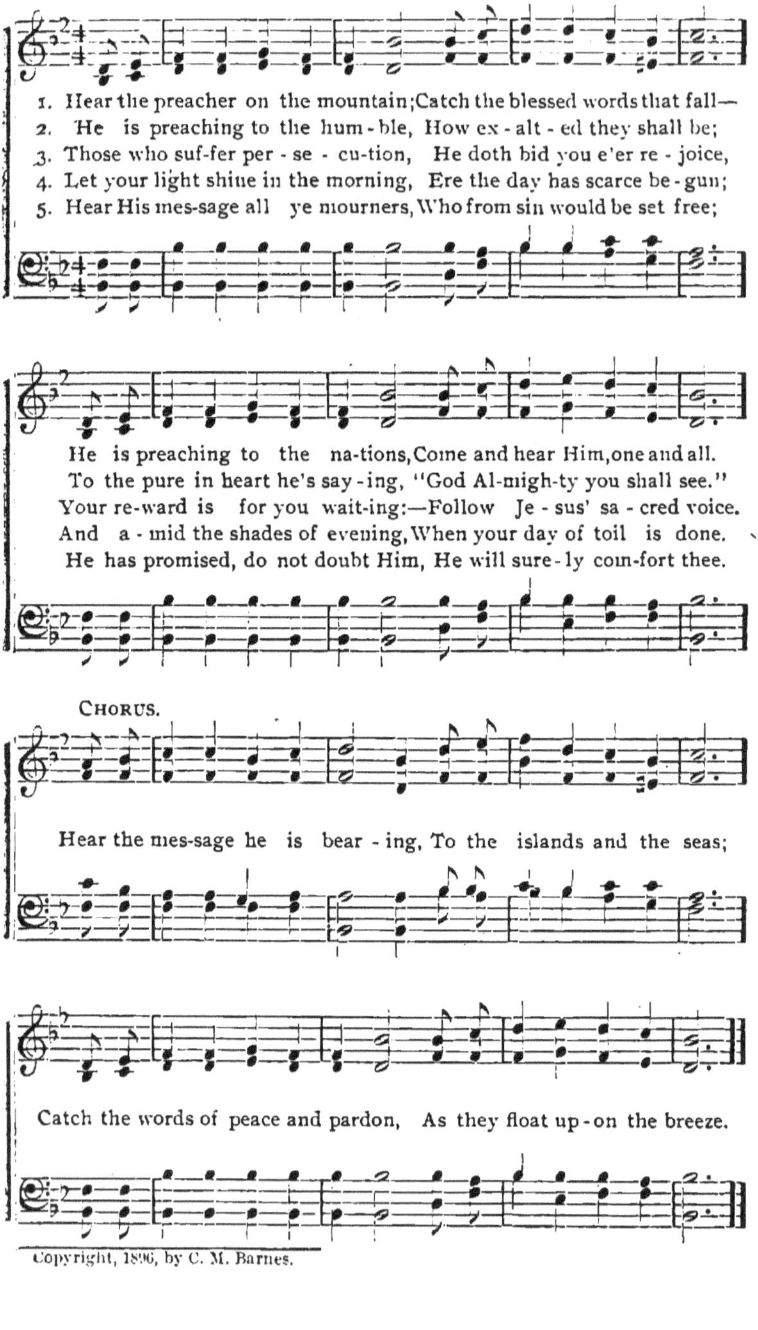

1. Hear the preacher on the mountain; Catch the blessed words that fall—
2. He is preaching to the hum-ble, How ex-alt-ed they shall be;
3. Those who suf-fer per-se-cu-tion, He doth bid you e'er re-joice,
4. Let your light shine in the morning, Ere the day has scarce be-gun;
5. Hear His mes-sage all ye mourners, Who from sin would be set free;

He is preaching to the na-tions, Come and hear Him, one and all.
To the pure in heart he's say-ing, "God Al-migh-ty you shall see."
Your re-ward is for you wait-ing:—Follow Je-sus' sa-cred voice.
And a-mid the shades of evening, When your day of toil is done.
He has promised, do not doubt Him, He will sure-ly com-fort thee.

CHORUS.

Hear the mes-sage he is bear-ing, To the islands and the seas;

Catch the words of peace and pardon, As they float up-on the breeze.

Copyright, 1896, by C. M. Barnes.

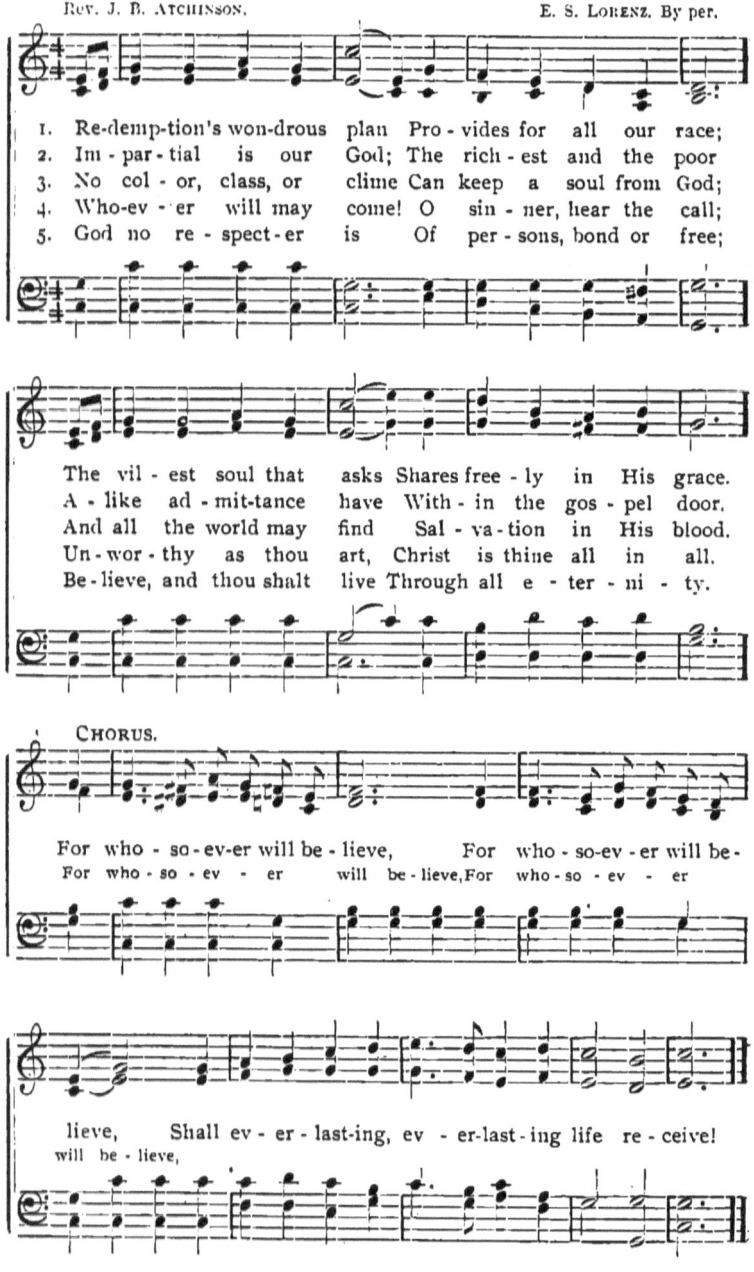

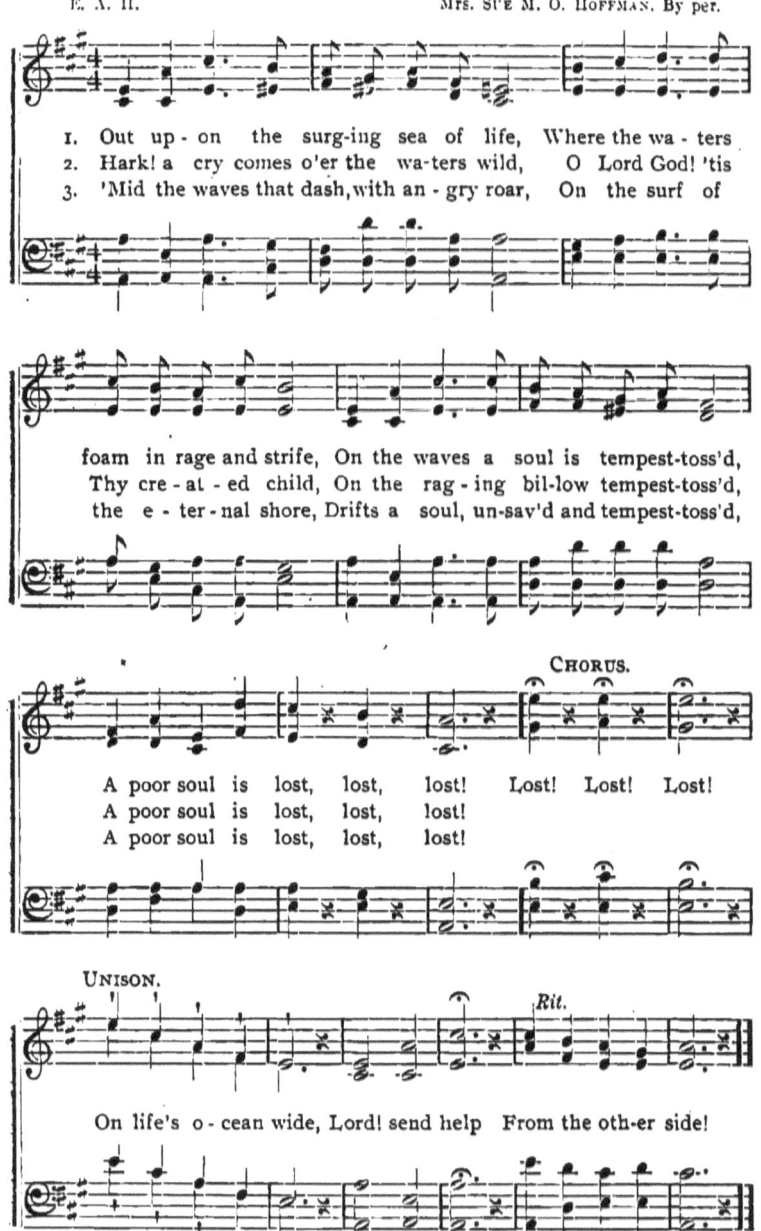

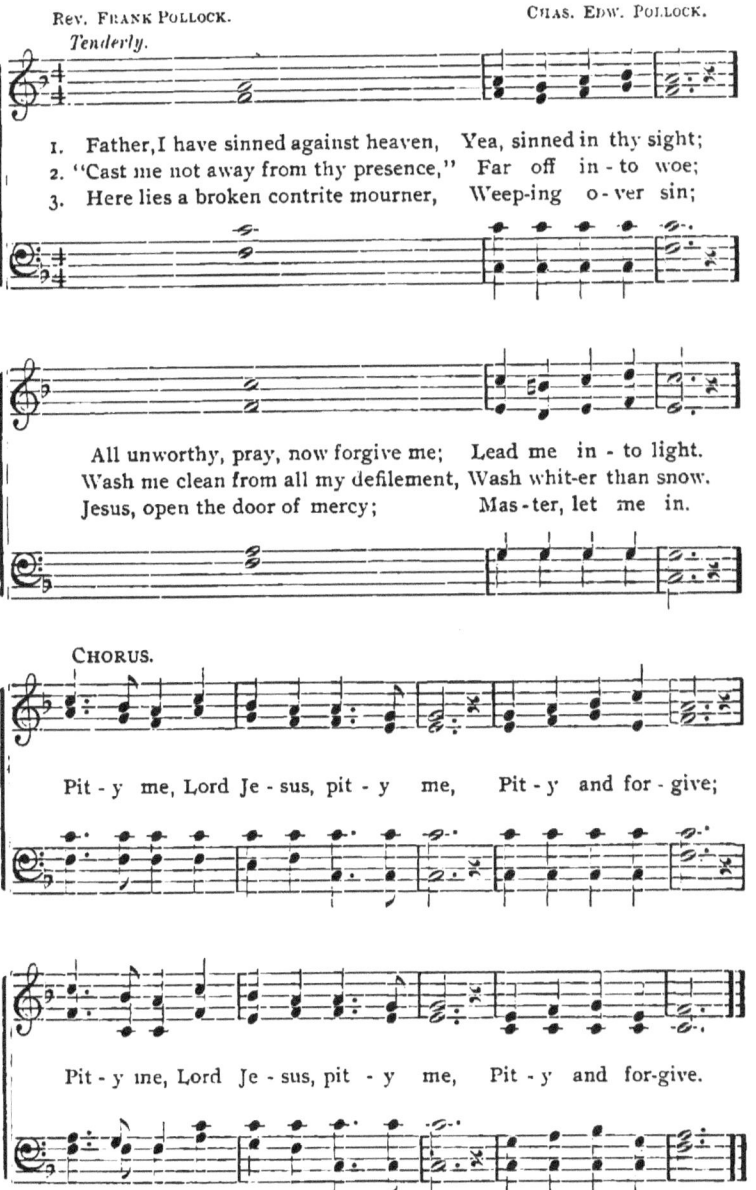

Over and Over—Concluded.

o-ver a-gain, Tell them of Jesus the Savior of men— Pleadingly, earnestly, lov-ing-ly, ten-der-ly, Tell them of Jesus the Savior.

No. 29. What a Friend.

JOSEPH SCRIVEN. 1855.　　　　　　　C. C. CONVERSE.

1. What a Friend we have in Jesus, All our sins and griefs to bear!
What a privilege to carry Ev'rything to God in prayer!
Oh, what peace we often forfeit, Oh, what needless pain we bear,
D. S.—All because we do not carry Ev'rything to God in prayer!

2 Have we trials and temptations?
Is there trouble anywhere?
We should never be discouraged,
Take it to the Lord in prayer.
Can we find a Friend so faithful,
Who will all our sorrows share?
Jesus knows our every weakness,
Take it to the Lord in prayer.

3 Are we weak and heavy laden,
Cumbered with a load of care?
Precious Savior, still our refuge,—
Take it to the Lord in prayer.
Do thy friends despise, forsake thee?
Take it to the Lord in prayer;
In His arms He'll take and shield thee,
Thou wilt find a solace there.

No. 32. That Fair Land.

VESTER SMITH.   C. M. BARNES.

1. There's a land far a-way where the long sum-mer day, Ev-er clothed with a splen-dor so fair, 'Tis a man-sion of rest for the good and the blest—And we'll meet all the loved o-ver there.
2. In that land of the blest, with its glo-ries confessed We shall rest with our Sav-ior a-bove; In that bright sunny clime as the stars we shall shine, Crown'd with glo-ry like an-gels of love.
3. Oh! that land fair and bright, 'tis a home of de-light, 'Tis a home where we'll rest ev-er-more; With a robe and a crown in that home of re-nown We shall sing with the loved gone be-fore.

CHORUS.

O - ver there,   o - ver there,   We shall meet with the pure and the fair,   O-ver there,
O - ver there, o - ver there, We shall meet by and by, We shall meet with the pure and the fair, O-ver there, o - ver there, We shall meet

Copyright, 1896, by C. M. Barnes.

That Fair Land—Concluded.

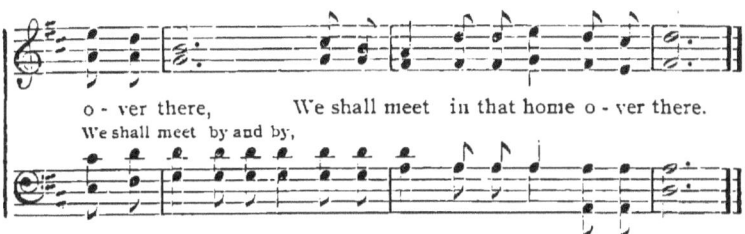

No. 33. Youthful Consecration.

Anon.
CHAS. EDW. POLLOCK. By per.
With expression.

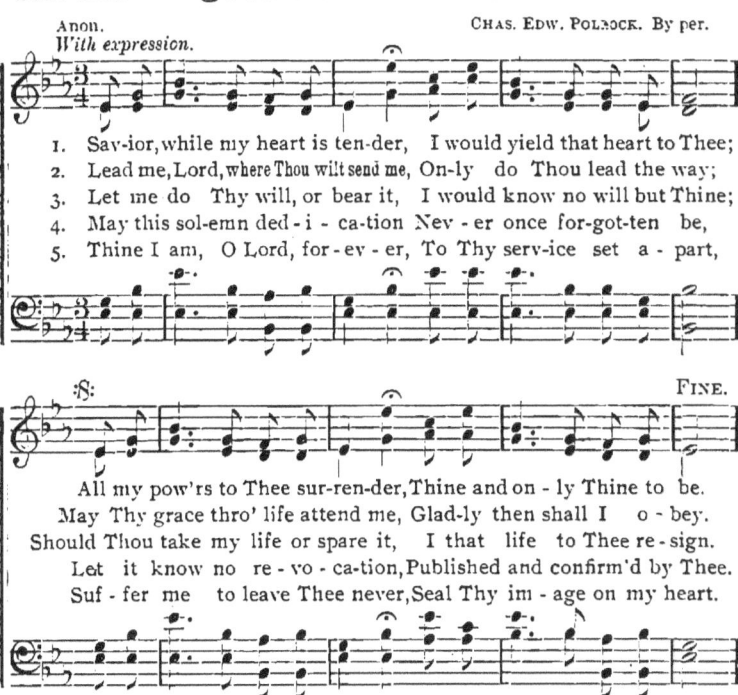

1. Sav-ior, while my heart is ten-der, I would yield that heart to Thee;
2. Lead me, Lord, where Thou wilt send me, On-ly do Thou lead the way;
3. Let me do Thy will, or bear it, I would know no will but Thine;
4. May this sol-emn ded-i-ca-tion Nev-er once for-got-ten be,
5. Thine I am, O Lord, for-ev-er, To Thy serv-ice set a-part,

All my pow'rs to Thee sur-ren-der, Thine and on-ly Thine to be.
May Thy grace thro' life attend me, Glad-ly then shall I o-bey.
Should Thou take my life or spare it, I that life to Thee re-sign.
Let it know no re-vo-ca-tion, Published and confirm'd by Thee.
Suf-fer me to leave Thee never, Seal Thy im-age on my heart.

D. S.—*Thy de-vot-ed servant make me, Fill my soul with love di-vine.*

Take me now, Lord Je-sus, take me, Let my youth-ful heart be Thine;

Copyright, 1887, by W. E. Penn.

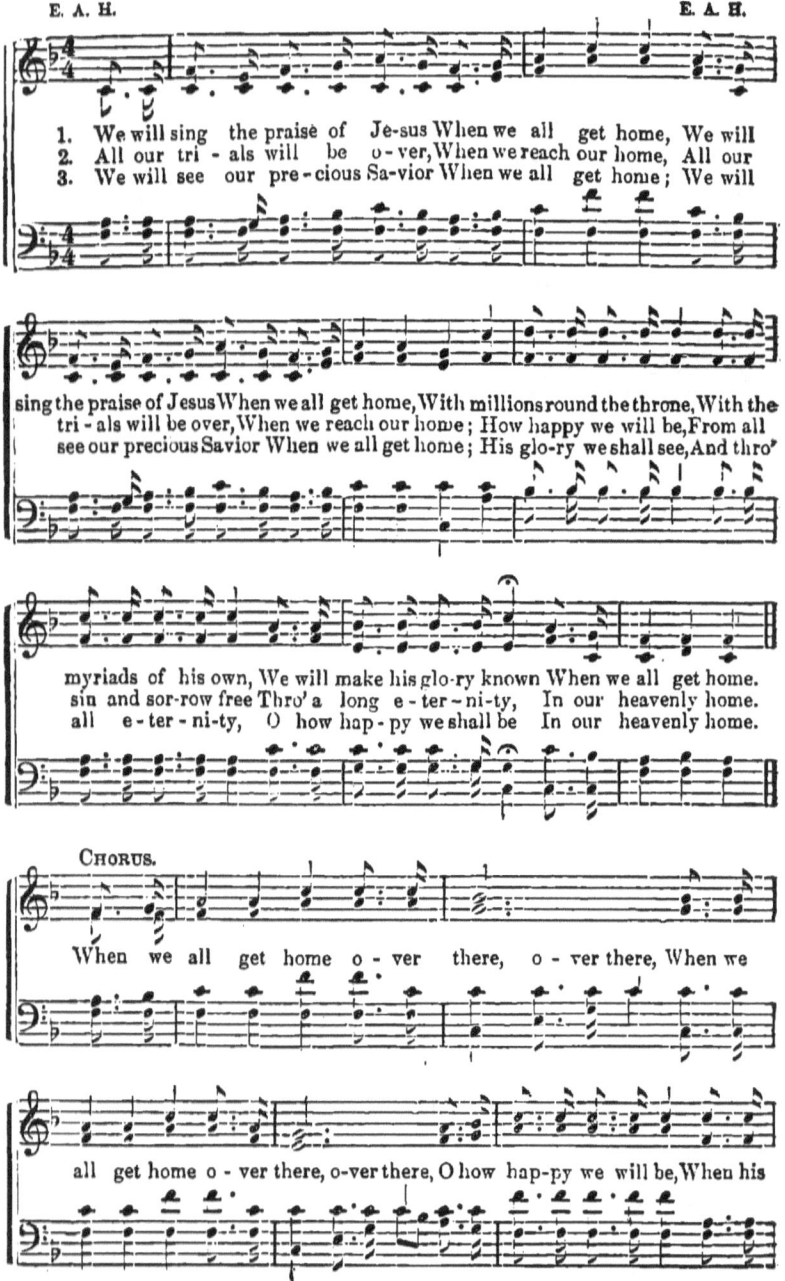

When We All Get Home.—Concluded.

glo - ry we shall see, When we all get home, o - ver there, o - ver there.

No. 35. There is a Fountain.

WM. COOPER.   Western Melody.

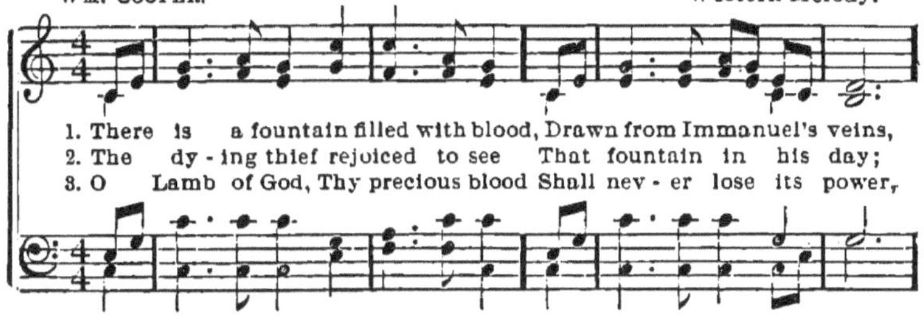

1. There is a fountain filled with blood, Drawn from Immanuel's veins,
2. The dy - ing thief rejoiced to see That fountain in his day;
3. O Lamb of God, Thy precious blood Shall nev - er lose its power,

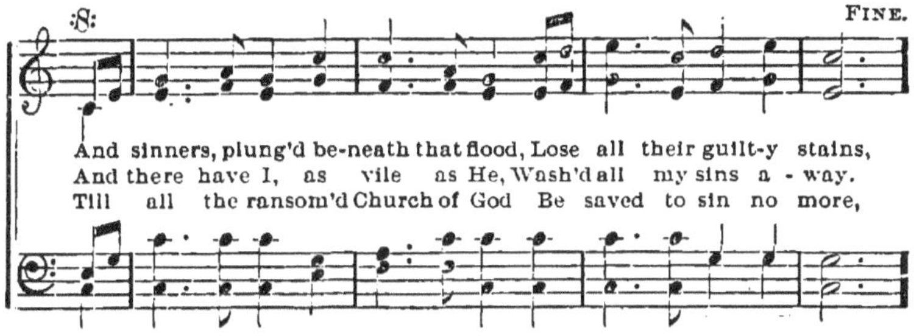

And sinners, plung'd be-neath that flood, Lose all their guilt-y stains,
And there have I, as vile as He, Wash'd all my sins a - way.
Till all the ransom'd Church of God Be saved to sin no more,

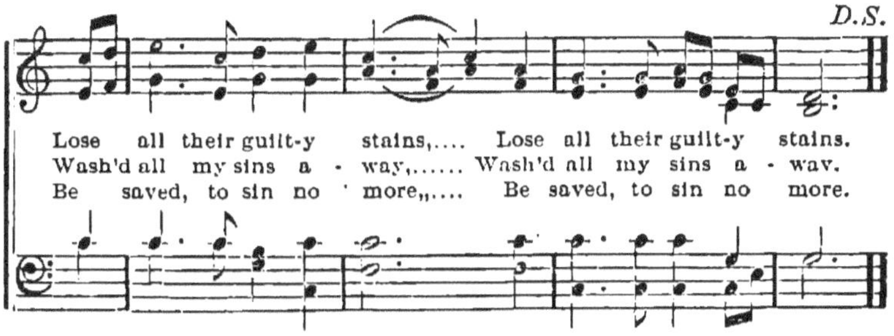

Lose all their guilt-y stains,.... Lose all their guilt-y stains.
Wash'd all my sins a - way,...... Wash'd all my sins a - way.
Be saved, to sin no more,,.... Be saved, to sin no more.

4 E'er since by faith I saw the stream
   Thy flowing wounds supply,
   Redeeming love has been me theme,
   And shall be till I die.

5 And when this lisping, stammering
   Lies silent in the grave,   [tongue
   Then in a nobler, sweeter song
   I'll sing Thy power to save.

No. 36. Clinging to the Rock.

"He only is my rock and my salvation."—Psa. 62:2.

Selected.   CHAS. EDW. POLLOCK. By per.

1. When the tempest ra-ges high, (rag-es high,) Sailing o'er life's stormy sea, (storm-y sea,) Storm-y bil-lows I de-fy, (I de-fy,) If I then may on-ly be, (on-ly be,) Cling-ing to the Rock.
2. When 'mid drifting wrecks I'm cast, (wrecks I'm cast,) Darkness setling thick a-round, (thick around,) Hope shall lift her light at last, (light at last,) If I then be on-ly found, (on-ly found.) Cling-ing to the Rock.
3. When the conqu'ring waves shall close, (waves shall close,) Proudly o'er me as I die, (as I die,) O-ver these brief vic-tor foes, (vic-tor foes,) I shall triumph by and by, (by and by,) Cling-ing to the Rock.

CHORUS.

Clinging to the Rock, Clinging to the Rock, I shall tri - umph still by and by, Cling - ing to the Rock.
I shall triumph by and by, I shall triumph by and by, Cling - ing, firm - ly cling-ing to the Rock.
Clinging, firmly clinging to the Rock.

Copyright, 1890, by W. E. Penn.

5 When the clouds of sorrow lower,
   And you need sustaining power,
   Then is faith's propitious hour;
   Then is the time to pray.

6 When the tempter is assailing,
   And your faith and hope are failing,
   Go to God with faith prevailing;
   Then is the time to pray.

7 When you feel your incompleteness,
   And the lack of heavenly meetness,
   You may find in Christ completeness;
   Then is the time to pray.

8 When you feel that death is nearing,
   Earth receding, disappearing,
   'Mid your trembling and your fearing,
   Then is the time to pray.

Copyright, 1894, by the Hoffman Music Co.

No. 44. The Gracious Invitation.

Rev. J. P. Kester, M. D.   Chas. Edw. Pollock.

1. Ho, thirst-y souls, draw near, The waters pure and free; Drink from life's sparkling fountain full, And ev-er hap-py be. The poor and rich may come And take the healing flood; Come, thirsty souls, no longer wait, There's life in Jesus' blood.

2. Yea, come, buy wine and milk, 'Twill life and strength impart; No long-er in thy weakness live, But strengthen now thine heart: "Whoso-ev-er will" may come And of this stream partake; Come hungry souls (oh, praise the Lord!) And eat for Jesus' sake.

3. My soul is full of bliss, This precious stream hath giv'n; Press on my soul to high-er joys, And gain the port of heav'n: Then round th' eternal throne, The song of triumph sing, While all the host of heav'n may join, To praise the Lord our King.

CHORUS.

Come, oh, come, Drink from life's. Ho, thirsty souls, draw near, The fountain full and free;

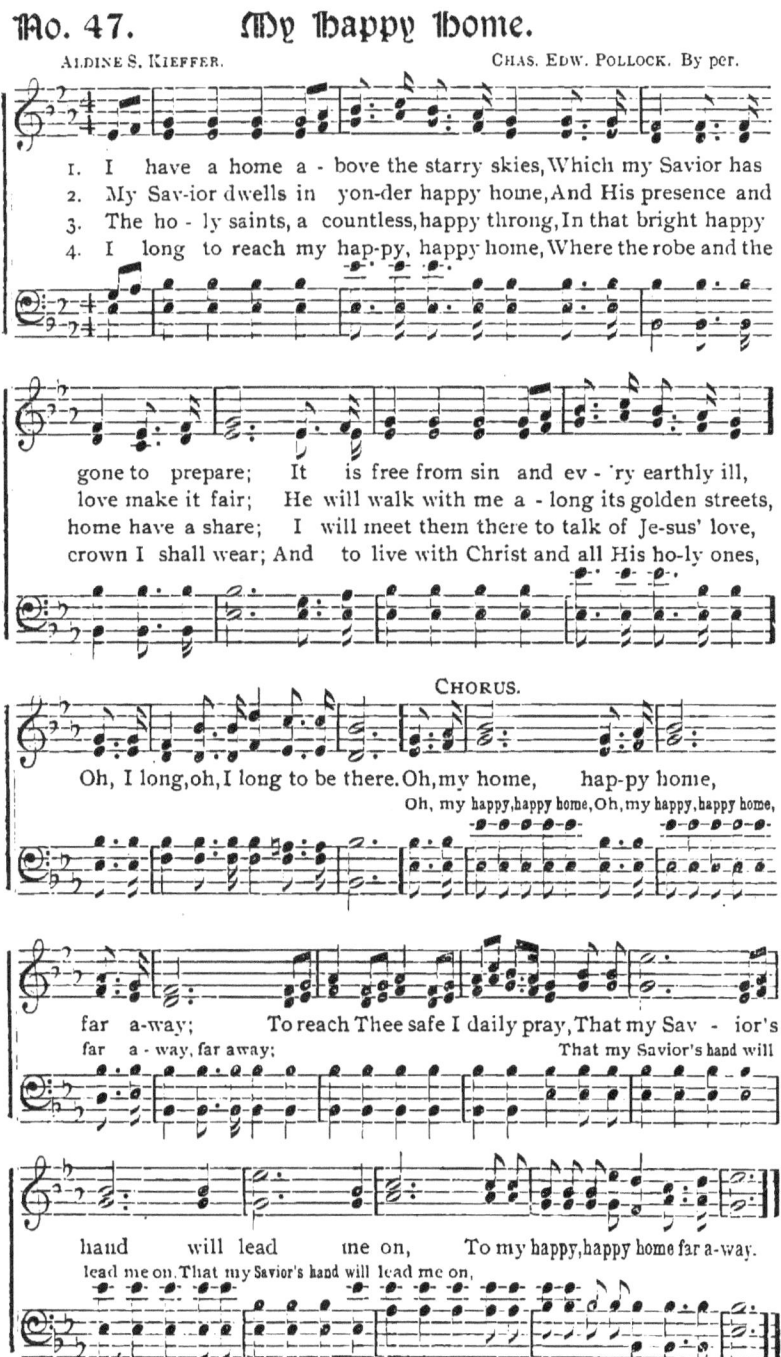

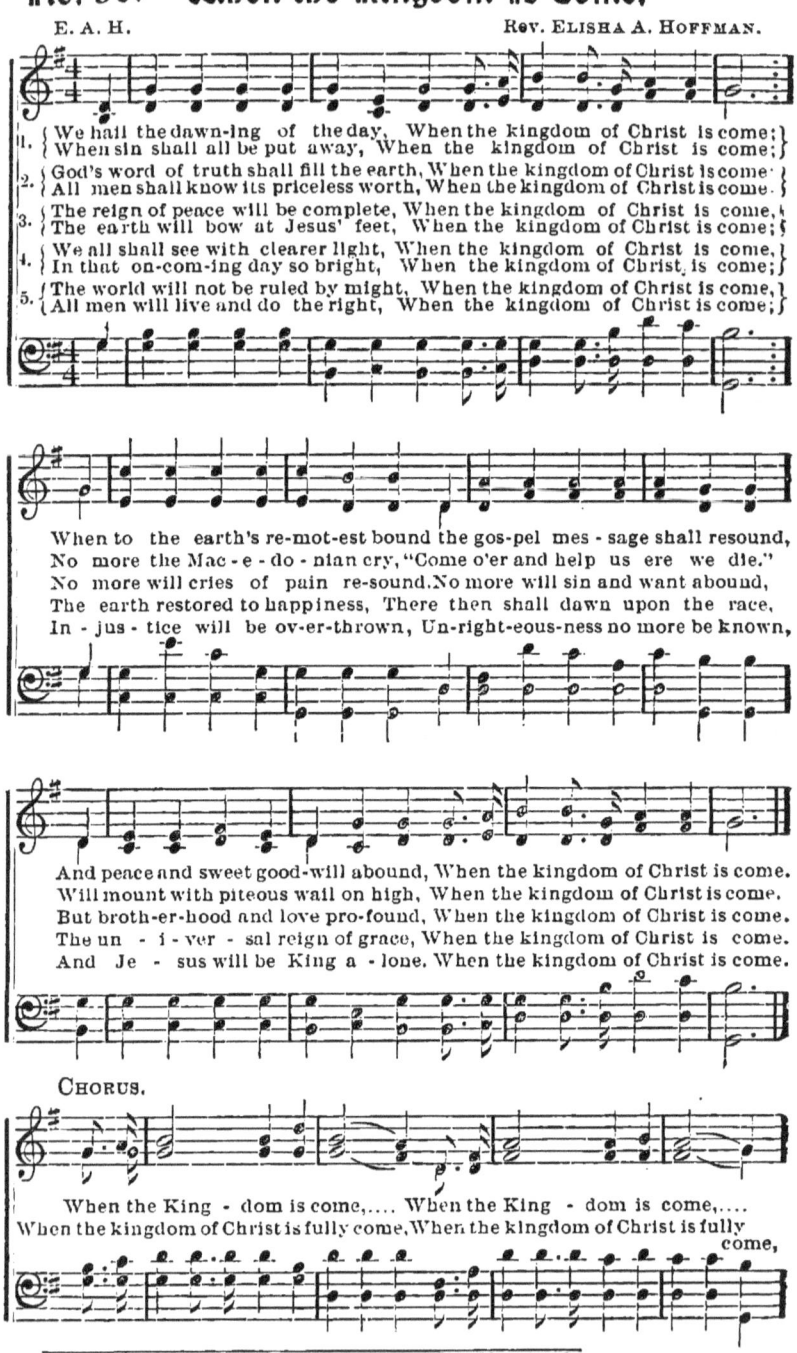

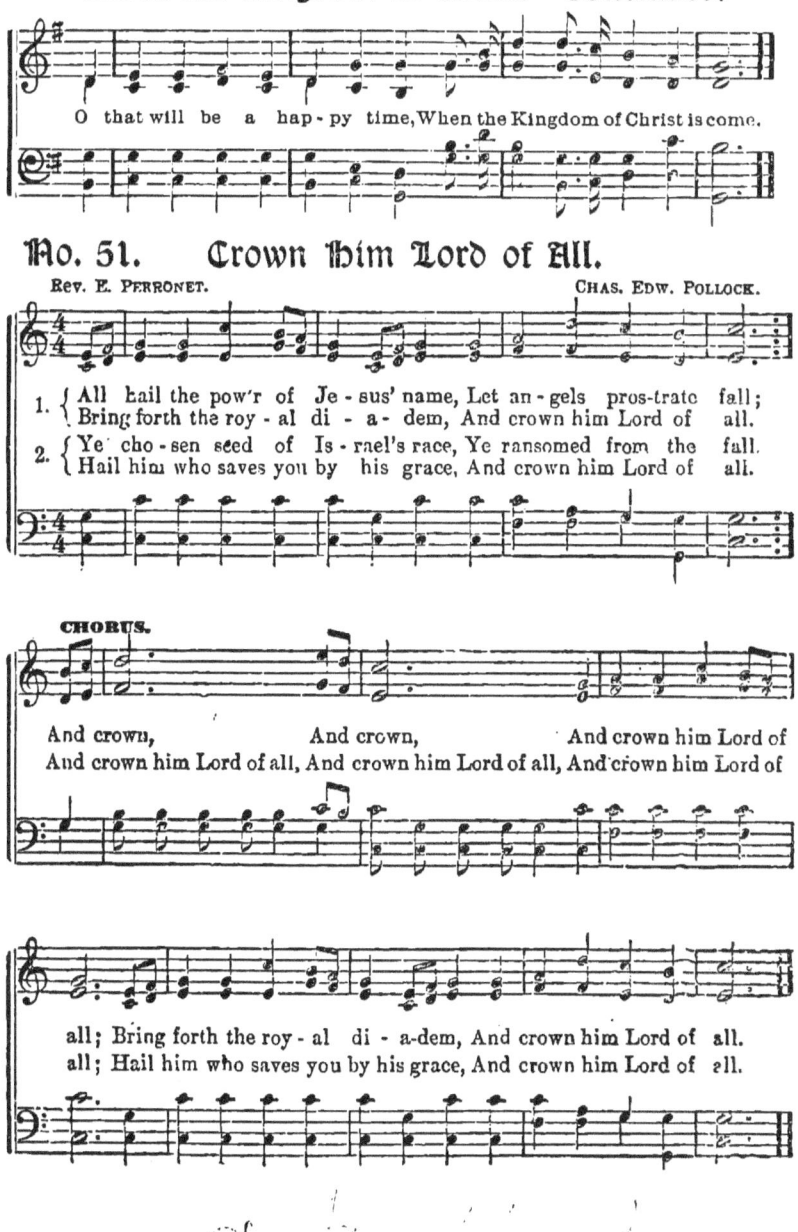

No. 53. Don't Keep Jesus Waiting.

E. A H. , Arranged.

Words and Arr. copyrighted, 1885, by THE HOFFMAN MUSIC Co., Cleveland.

No. 54. The Lost Soul's Lament.

Mrs. Lou. S. Bedford.   Jeremiah 8:20.   H. N. Lincoln.

1. The summer is end-ed, oh, God! And the har-vest for-ev-er past, While heedless life's ear-nest path I have trod, And now I'm un-done at last; With the best of "in-ten-tions" my path I have paved, But the harvest is passed and my soul is not saved.

2. The dews of God's grace have come down, Thro' the spring and the summer eves The beau-ti-ful rays of Au-tumn's bright sun Have rip-ened full ma-ny sheaves; All the while with vain dreamings my way I have paved, Till the summer is end-ed and I am not saved.

3. Full oft-en His "still" gentle voice, Has en-cour-aged my wayward heart To choose, in the place of life's fleet-ing joys, Like Ma-ry, "that bet-ter part," But a-las! ev-'ry warn-ing my proud heart has braved, The sum-mer is end-ed and I am not saved.

4. I tho't "there is time e-nough yet!" And the way was so strangely bright; I dreamed not the sun was quite so near set, I woke and be-held 'twas night! All the claims of the gos-pel a-las! I had waived Till the sheaves were all garnered and I am not saved.

5. I stretch out my weak helpless hand Far, far to-ward the jas-per sea, And pray one glimpse of that ra-di-ant land—Where lov-ing friends wait for me; Whose kind, faithful warnings, I oft-en have brav'd, But the harvest is end-ed and I am not saved.

From "Song Land Messenger." By per. of H. N. Lincoln, owner of Copyright.

No. 56. Church of God, Awake!

Mrs. EMILY J. BUGBEE. T. C. O'KANE. By per.

1. Church of God, whose conqu'ring banners Float along the glorious years,
2. In your cost-ly tem-ples praying, "Let Thy kingdom come, we pray,"
3. Grace and glo-ry He hath sent you, Cast your line in plac-es fair;
4. Shake the earth and rend the heaven, Wake thy sleeping children, Lord,

Gath'ring harvest rich and gold-en, Sowed in pov-er-ty and tears,
Are but words of i-dle meaning, If with these we turn a-way.
Scatter blessings *now*, He bids you, O'er His green earth ev'ry-where,
Till the measure full and e-ven Has been render'd at Thy word.

On-ward press the cross is bending Far to-ward the morning skies,
Boundless wealth to you is giv-en From His hand who ownes it all,
Till the millions in the twi-light Of the far off O-rient land,
Then from out her chrism of sor-row Shall the earth redeem'd a-rise,

Speed-y dawn of light por-tend-ing: Church of God, a-wake! a-rise!
And His eye be-holds in heav-en What ye render back for all.
In the gracious morning splendor, Of the gospel light shall stand.
And the fair mil-len-nial mor-row Dawn with o-pal-tint-ed skies.

From "Missionary Advocate."

Church of God, Awake!—Concluded.

CHORUS.

Church of God, . . . awake! a-rise! Christ, your Head . . and Master,
Church of God, a - wake! a - rise! Christ, your Head and

cries, Send the Gos-pel's joyful sound Unto earth's remotest bound.
Mas-ter,cries,Oh, send the Gos - pel's joy-ful sound

No. 57. Nettleton. 8s. 7s. D.

ROBERT ROBINSON. 1757. J. WYETH'S COLL. 1812.

FINE.

1. { Come, thou fount of ev-'ry bless-ing, Tune my heart to sing Thy grace; }
   { Streams of mer-cy nev-er ceas-ing, Call for songs of loudest praise: }
D. C.—Praise the mount,—O fix me on it, Mount of God's un-chang-ing love.

D. C.

Teach me some me - lo-dious sonnet, Sung by flam-ing tongues above;

2 Here I raise my Ebenezer;
    Hither by Thy help I'm come;
  And I hope, by Thy good pleasure,
    Safely to arrive at home:
  Jesus sought me when a stranger,
    Wandering from the fold of God;
  He to save my soul from danger,
    Interposed His precious blood.

3 O to grace how great a debtor
    Daily I'm constrained to be!
  Let that grace, Lord, like a fetter,
    Bind my wandering heart to Thee.
  Prone to wander, Lord, I feel it;
    Prone to leave the God I love;
  Here's my heart; Lord, take and seal it;
    Seal it from Thy courts above.

No. 58. Working for the Crown.

Mrs. H. A. Mabry. H. A. R. Horton.

1. Shall I be content with one star in my crown, When heaven's bright portals I see! The answer comes back—strive a cluster to win, And the way will be brighter for thee.
2. When, Lord, must I work? shall I go in the heat, To white and to wide harvest fields, Where work is so great and the labor'rs so few, And the promise a bountiful yield?
3. Yes, all kinds of work I will find in this field, My task then quite plain I can see, And now having found it I'll labor and wait, For wholly Thine, Lord, would I be.
4. And how shall I get these rare gems for my crown? Must I wait till heaven I gain? Yes, yes, but toil here for the Master's renown, Day by day for the Lamb that was slain.

CHORUS.

Working for the crown, ... Working for the crown, for the crown, ...
for the beautiful golden crown, Working for the crown, for the beautiful golden crown,

Copyright, 1889, by H. A. R. Horton. Used by per.

No. 60. Shall We Find Them at the Portals?

In Memory of Walter N. Rankin.

J. E. RANKIN, D. D.   E. S. LORENZ. By per.

1. Will they meet us, cheer, and greet us, Those we've loved, who've gone be-fore?
2. Hearts are bro-ken for some to-ken, That they live, and love us yet;
3. And we oft-en, as days soften, And comes out the evening star,
4. Past yon por-tals, our im-mor-tals, Those who walk with him in white;

Shall we find them at the por-tals, Find our beau-ti-fied im-mor-tals,
And we ask, "Can those who've left us, Of love's look and tone bereft us,
Looking west-ward, sit and wonder, Whether, when so far a-sun-der,
Do they, 'mid their bliss, re-call us? Know they what events be-fall us?

D. S.—*We shall find them at the portals, Find our beau-ti-fied im-mor-tals,*

FINE.   CHORUS.

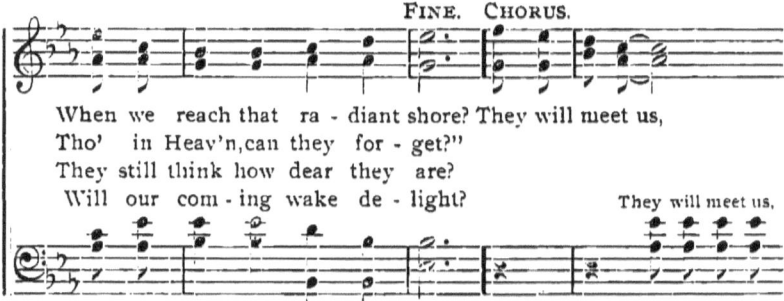

When we reach that ra-diant shore? They will meet us,
Tho' in Heav'n, can they for-get?"
They still think how dear they are?
Will our com-ing wake de-light?   They will meet us,

When we reach that ra-diant shore.

No. 61. Beautiful Stream.

Anon. CHAS. EDW. POLLOCK. By per.

1. Oh, have you not heard of the beau-ti-ful stream, That flows thro' our Father's land, It's wa-ters gleam bright in a heav-en-ly light, And rip-ple o'er gold-en sand.
2. This beau-ti-ful stream is the riv-er of Life, It flows for all na-tions free, A balm for each wound in its wa-ters are found, O sin-ner, it flows for thee.
3. Oh, will you not drink of the beau-ti-ful stream, And dwell on its peaceful shore? The Spir-it says "Come, all ye wea-ry ones home, And wan-der in sin no more.

CHORUS.

O beau-ti-ful stream, . . . Riv-er of pleasures di-vine, ... Its waters gleam bright with its heav-en-ly light, O beau-ti-ful stream.

O beau-ti-ful, beau-ti-ful, beau-ti-ful stream, Riv-er of pleasures, of pleasures divine, O beau-ti-ful, beau-ti-ful stream.

No. 63. I Am the Lord's Forever.

E. A. H.   E. A. HOFFMAN.

1. My gladsome heart these words repeat; "I am the Lord's forever!" And every time they seem more sweet; Oh, praise his name forever!
2. Too long and far from Christ I strayed, But he forsook me never; Now walking in the narrow way, I am the Lord's forever!
3. 'Twas Christ, the Lamb of Calvary, That loved and sought me ever, That broke my chains and set me free; Oh, praise his name forever!
4. I am the Lord's! O blessed thought! And he will leave me never; By Jesus' blood my soul was bought, And I am his forever!
5. This is the burden of my song; "I am the Lord's forever!" And naught that earth can offer me My heart from Christ can sever.

Chorus.

Hallelujah! hallelujah! Hallelujah! hallelujah! Light breaks in upon my soul; Jesus' blood has made me whole!

COPYRIGHTED 1883, BY E. A. HOFFMAN.

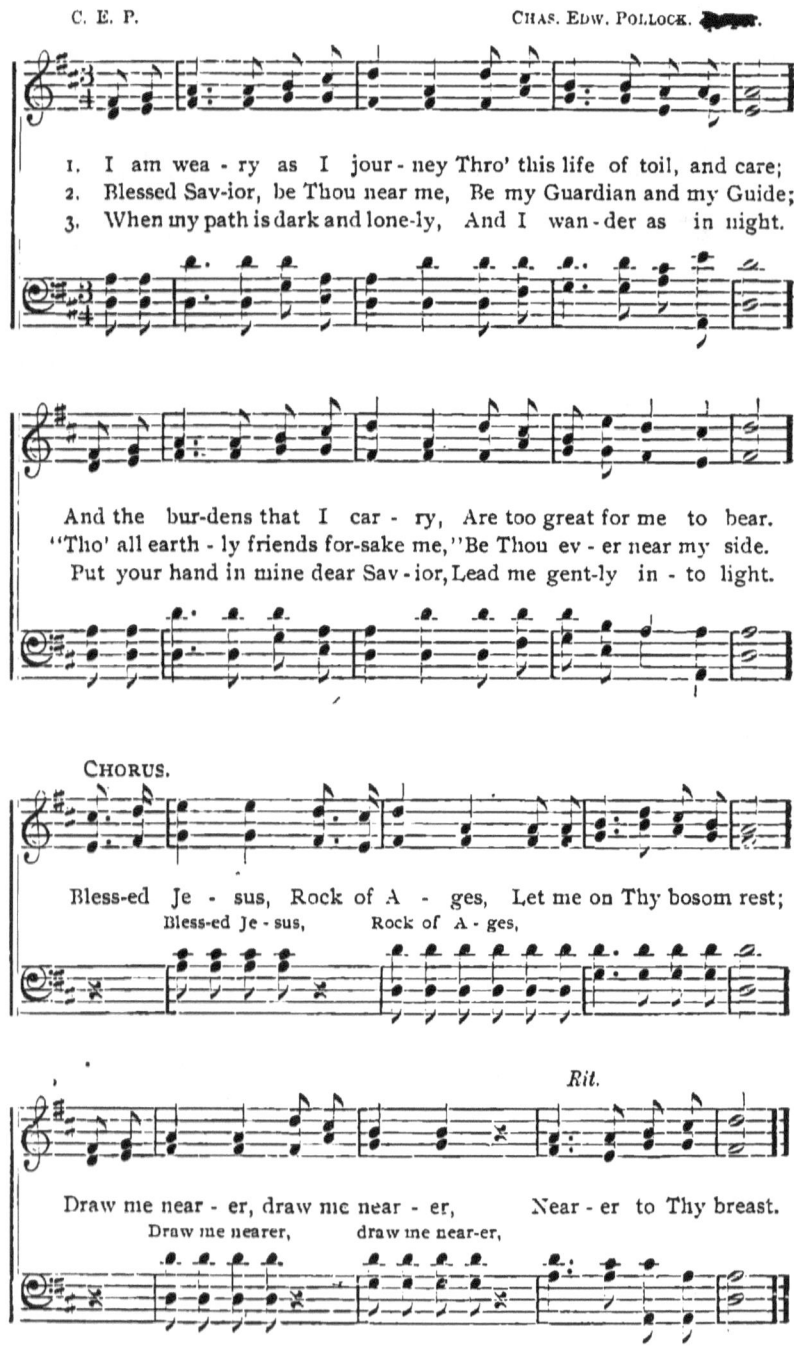

No. 67. Say, Are You Ready?

A. S. KIEFFER. T. C. O'KANE.

1. Should the death angel knock at thy chamber, In the still watch of to-night,
2. Ma-ny sad spir-its now are de-part-ing In-to the world of despair;
3. Ma-ny redeemed ones now are ascending In-to the mansions of light;

Say, will your spirit pass in-to torment, Or to the land of de-light?
Ev-'ry brief moment brings your doom nearer; Sinner, O sinner, be-ware!
Je-sus is pleading high up in glo-ry, Seek-ing to save you to-night.

CHORUS.

Say, are you ready, oh! are you ready, If the death angel should call?

Say, are you read-y? oh! are you read-y? Mercy stands waiting for all.

From "Jasper and Gold," by per.

No. 71. Crown, Harp and Song.

Words and music written at Kansas City, Mo., April, 1888.

F. A. BLACKMER. H. N. LINCOLN.

Moderato.

1. I would do each du-ty here I would fight and nev-er fear,
   And when past these scenes of strife, I shall then a *crown* of life,
   And the cross would meekly bear; With the ransomed ev-er wear.

2. I would fol-low Je-sus now, At His feet would humbly bow,
   And with Him I soon shall stand, With a *harp* with-in my hand,
   Nev-er seek-ing earthly fame; Harp-ing prais-es to His name.

3. To the Father and the Son, Who such wondrous things have done,
   I would sing thro' endless days, *Songs* of ev-er-last-ing praise,
   For a lost and ru-ined race; For the gift of sav-ing grace.

CHORUS.

Oh, a star-ry crown to wear, Oh, a gold-en harp to bear, When be-fore the great I Am, All the might-y ransom'd throng, Swell the glad tri-umph-ant song, Song of Mo-ses and the Lamb.

From "Song Land Messenger," by per. of H. N. Lincoln, owner of Copyright.

No. 72. Am I a Soldier?

"Endure hardness as a good soldier of Jesus Christ."—2 Tim. 2:3.
Uniting with the Church, to be used when inviting the Candidates to come forward.

Rev. I. WATTS, D. D.

1. Am I a Sol-dier of the cross, A fol-'wer of the Lamb,
2. Are there no foes for me to face? Must I not stem the flood?
3. Thy Saints in all this glo-rious war Shall conquer, tho' they die;

And shall I fear to own His cause, Or blush to speak His name?
Is this vile world a friend to grace, To help me on to God?
They see the tri-umph from a-far, With faith's discerning eye,

Must I be car-ried to the skies, On flow-'ry beds of ease,
Sure I must fight if I would reign: In-crease my courage Lord!
When that il-lus-trious day shall rise, And all Thine ar-mies shine

While oth-ers fought to win the prize, And sail'd thro' bloody seas?
I'll bear the toil, en-dure the pain, Sup-port-ed by Thy word.
In robes of vic-tory thro' the skies, The glo-ry shall be Thine.

No. 73.   That's Enough for Me.

"I know there are many who seek for happiness in the pleasures of the world. I go to Jesus. He assures me that he loves and saves me, and that's enough for me." The testimony of an earnest, devoted Christian.

E. A. H.   Rev. Elisha A. Hoffman.

1. O, love sur-pass-ing knowledge! O, grace so full and free!
2. O, won-der-ful sal-va-tion, That I should ransomed be!
3. O, blood of Christ so pre-cious, That flows from Cal-va-ry!
4. O, won-drous love of Je-sus! What love could sweeter be?
5. We live in sweet com-mun-ion, In bless-ed har-mo-ny;

I know that Je-sus loves me, And that's e-nough for me.
'Tis mine, this sweet as-sur-ance, And that's e-nough for me.
It cleans-es me com-plete-ly, And that's e-nough for me.
He keeps me saved and hap-py, And that's e-nough for me.
This, this is full sal-va-tion, And that's e-nough for me.

REFRAIN.

And that's e-nough for me, E-nough of joy for me;

I know that Je-sus loves me, And that's e-nough for me.
'Tis mine, this sweet as-sur-ance, And that's e-nough for me.
It cleans-es me com-plete-ly, And that's e-nough for me.
He keeps me saved and hap-py, And that's e-nough for me.
God's free and full sal-va-tion, Oh, that's e-nough for me.

6 The worldling seeks for pleasure,
In earthly vanity;
My treasures are in heaven,
And that's enough for me.
Cho. And that's enough for me,
Enough of joy for me;
My treasures are in heaven,
And that's enough for me.

7 When ends our toil and sorrow,
A better home I'll see,
And be with Christ forever,
And that's enough for me.
Cho. And that's enough for me,
Enough of joy for me;
To be with Christ forever,
Oh, that's enough for me!

Copyright, 1878, 1887, 1893, by the Hoffman Music Co.

No. 79. Tell It to Jesus Alone.

J. E. Rankin, D. D.   "Tell it to Jesus."—Matt. 14:12.   Rev. E. S. Lorenz.

1. Are you wea-ry, are you heav-y heart-ed? Tell it to Je-sus,
2. Do the tears flow down your cheeks unbidden? Tell it to Je-sus,
3. Do you fear the gath'ring clouds of sor-row? Tell it to Je-sus,
4. Are you troub-led at the tho't of dy-ing? Tell it to Je-sus.

Tell it to Je-sus. Are you grieving o-ver joys de-part-ed?
Tell it to Je-sus. Have you sins that to man's eyes are hid-den?
Tell it to Je-sus. Are you anx-ious what shall be to-mor-row?
Tell it to Je-sus. For Christ's coming Kingdom are you sigh-ing?

CHORUS.

Tell it to Je-sus a-lone. Tell it to Je-sus, Tell it to Je-sus, He is a friend that's well known; You have no other such a friend or broth-er; Tell it to Je-sus a-lone.

From "Songs of Refreshing," by per.

Beyond the Swelling Flood—Concluded.

No. 81.   Greenville.   8s and 7s.

Rev. R. Robinson. 1758.   J. J. Rousseau.

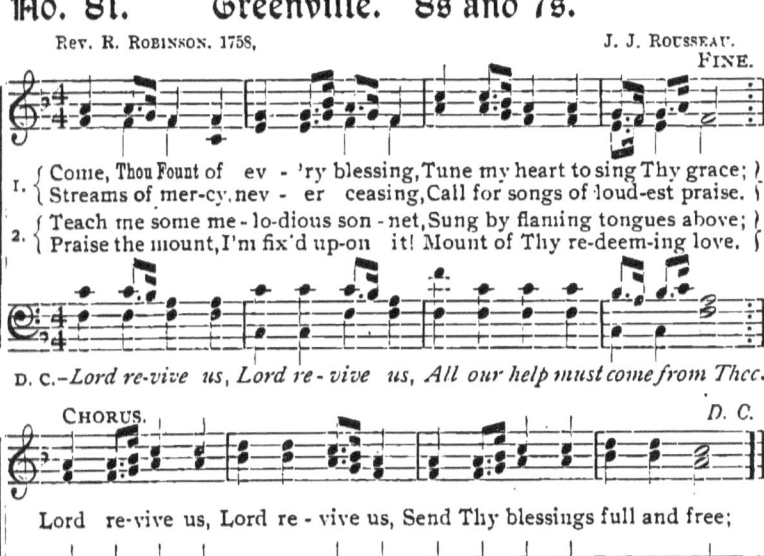

1. { Come, Thou Fount of ev - 'ry blessing, Tune my heart to sing Thy grace; }
   { Streams of mer-cy, nev - er ceasing, Call for songs of loud-est praise. }
2. { Teach me some me - lo-dious son - net, Sung by flaming tongues above; }
   { Praise the mount, I'm fix'd up-on it! Mount of Thy re-deem-ing love. }

D. C.—*Lord re-vive us, Lord re-vive us, All our help must come from Thee.*

CHORUS.

Lord re-vive us, Lord re-vive us, Send Thy blessings full and free;

3 Here I raise my Ebenezer,
   Hither by Thy help I've come;
   And I hope, by Thy good pleasure,
   Safely to arrive at home.

4 Jesus sought me, when a stranger,
   Wand'ring from the fold of God;
   He to rescue me from danger,
   Interposed His precious blood.

5 Oh, to grace how great a debtor,
   Daily I'm constrained to be!
   Let Thy goodness, like a fetter,
   Bind my wand'ring heart to Thee.

6 Prone to wander, Lord, I feel it,
   Prone to leave the God I love—
   Here's my heart, oh, take and seal it,
   Seal it for Thy courts above.

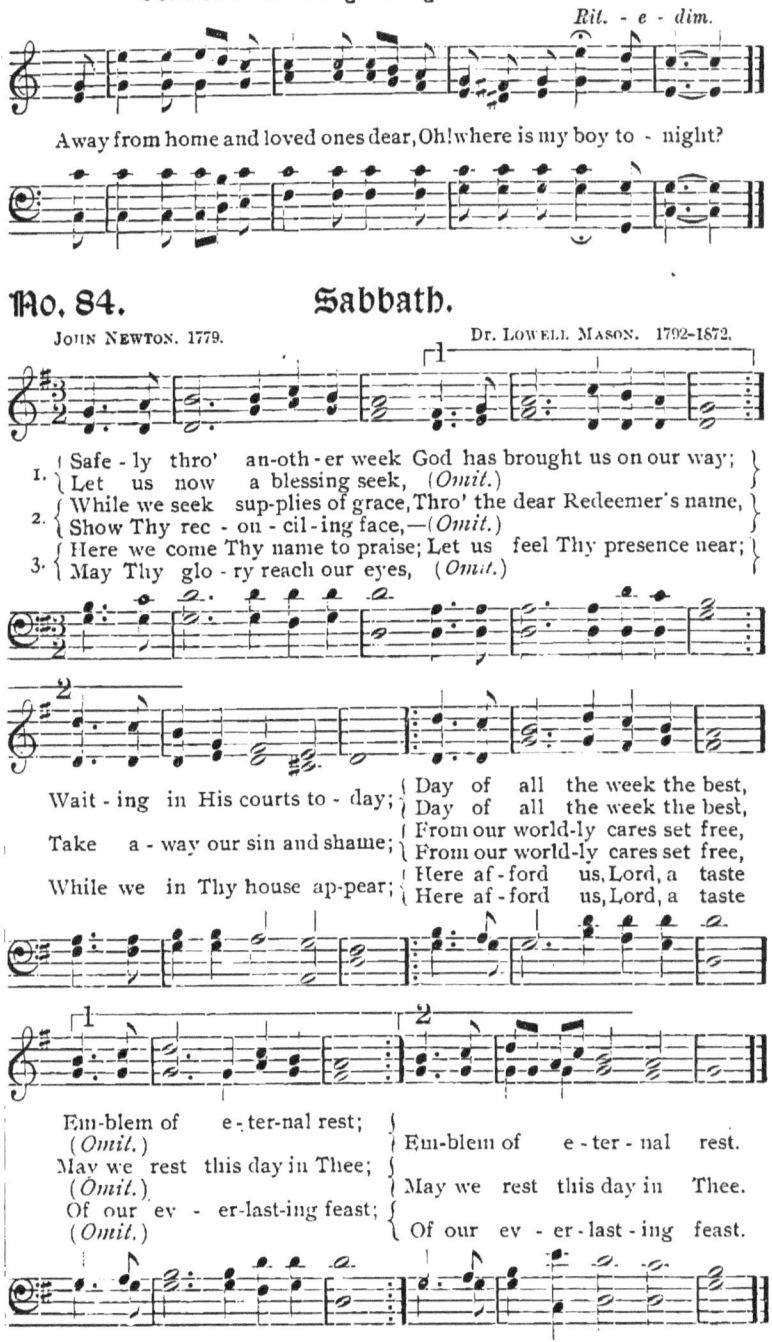

No. 85.   My Home Above.

LOUISA E.   CHAS. EDW. POLLOCK. By per.

1. I love to think of my home above, In the glorious realms of light,
2. I love to think of my home above, Of that pure and ho-ly clime,
3. I love to think of my home above, Of the angel forms so bright,
4. Sweet-est of all is the tho't of Him, Who did leave His throne on high,
5. That in that beau-ti-ful home above I may have a man-sion fair;

Of the pear-ly gates and the golden streets, In the land where there is no night.
Where the sorrows of earth can never come, But eternal joys will be mine.
Of the blessed ones there around the throne, In the land of pure delight.
And did come to this sinful world of ours To suffer, and bleed, and die.
And my heart is full of joy and praise, For I know that my treasure is there.

CHORUS.

Home, sweet home! Happy home, sweet home! Oh, say, will you
Home, sweet home, Home, sweet home,   Home, sweet home, hap-py, home, sweet home,

No. 88. When I See the Blood.

"When I see the blood I will pass over you."—Ex. 12:13.
"Christ our passover is sacrificed for us."—1 Chor. 5:7.

JOHN.   J. G. F.

1. Christ our Redeemer, died on the cross, Died for the sinner, paid all His due;
2. Chief-est of sin-ners, Je-sus can save, As He has promised so will He do;
3. Judgment is coming, all will be there, Who have rejected? who have refused?
4. Oh, what compassion, oh, boundless love, Jesus hath power, Je-sus is true;

All who receive Him, need never fear, For He will pass, will pass over you.
Oh, sinner, hear Him, trust in His word, Then He will pass, will pass over you.
Oh, sin-ner, hasten, let Je-sus in, Then He will pass, will pass over you.
All who believe, are safe from the storm, Oh, He will pass, will pass over you.

CHORUS.

When I see the blood, When I see the blood,
When I see the blood, When I see the blood.
When I see the blood, I will pass, I will pass over you.
When I see the blood, over you,

By Foote Bros., not copyrighted. Let no one do so. May this song ever be free to be published for the glory of God.

No. 89. One More Witness for Christ.

"For thou shalt be His witness unto all men."—Acts 22:15.

J. M. Hunt. J. M. Hunt. By per.

1. One more witness for Christ to-night, Holding His banner un-furled;
2. One more soul is redeemed from sin, Wash'd by the blood of the Lamb;
3. Help us, Savior, the vic-t'ry gain, Un-der Thy ban-ner of love;

One more sol-dier ar-rayed to fight, Bat-tling a-gainst the world.
One more heart that was toss'd within, Now has per - pet - ual calm.
Ev - er, then, shall we praise Thy name, And dwell with Thee above.

CHORUS.

Bless - ed Re-deem - er, Bless - ed Re-deem - er,
Blessed Redeemer, by Thee we will stand, Marching, if onward shall be the command,

Bless - - ed Re - deem - er, We'll give the praise to Thee.
Ev - er un-furled shall Thy ban - ner be;

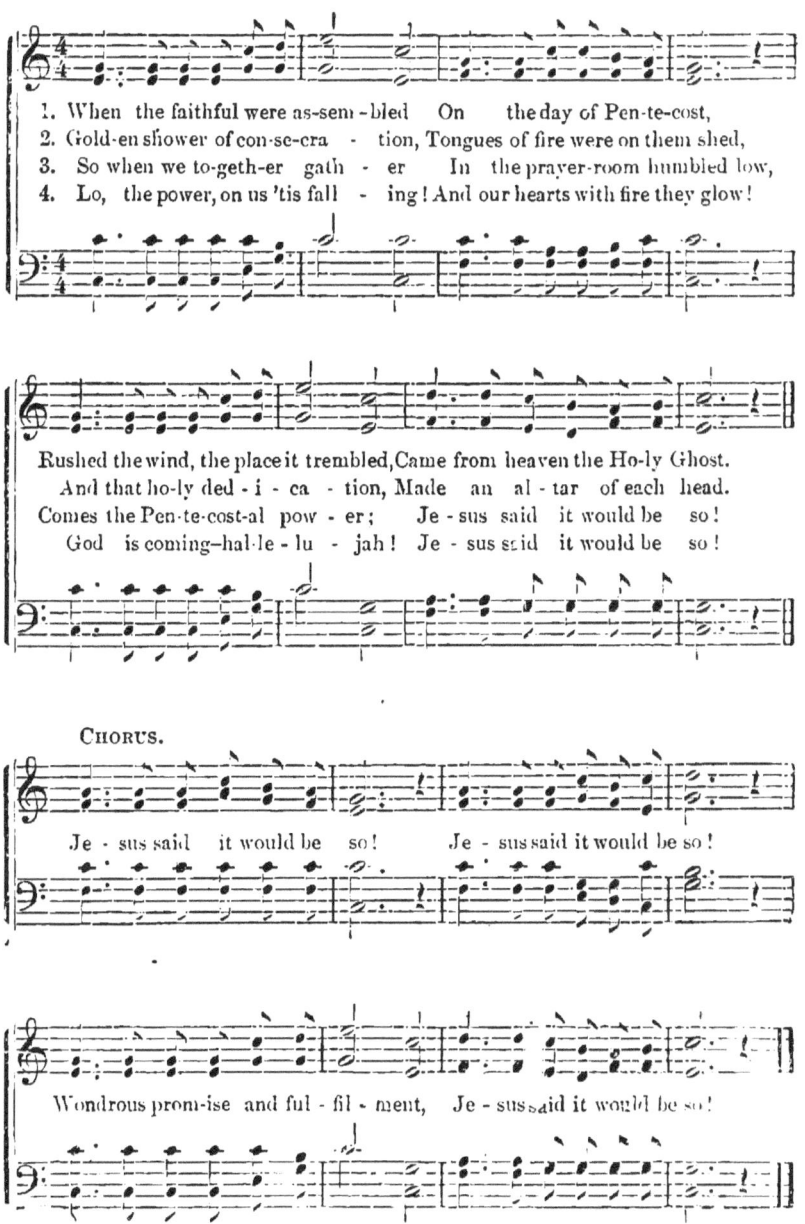

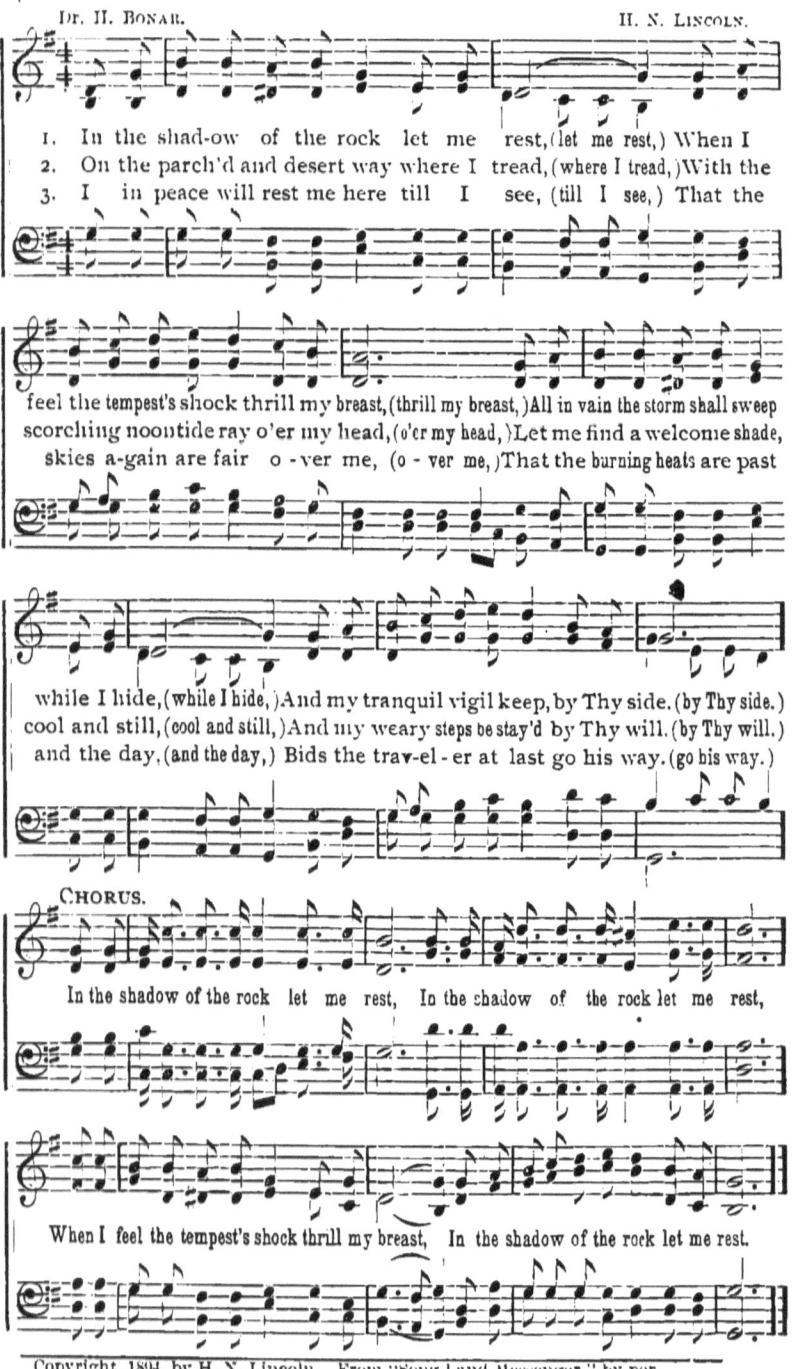

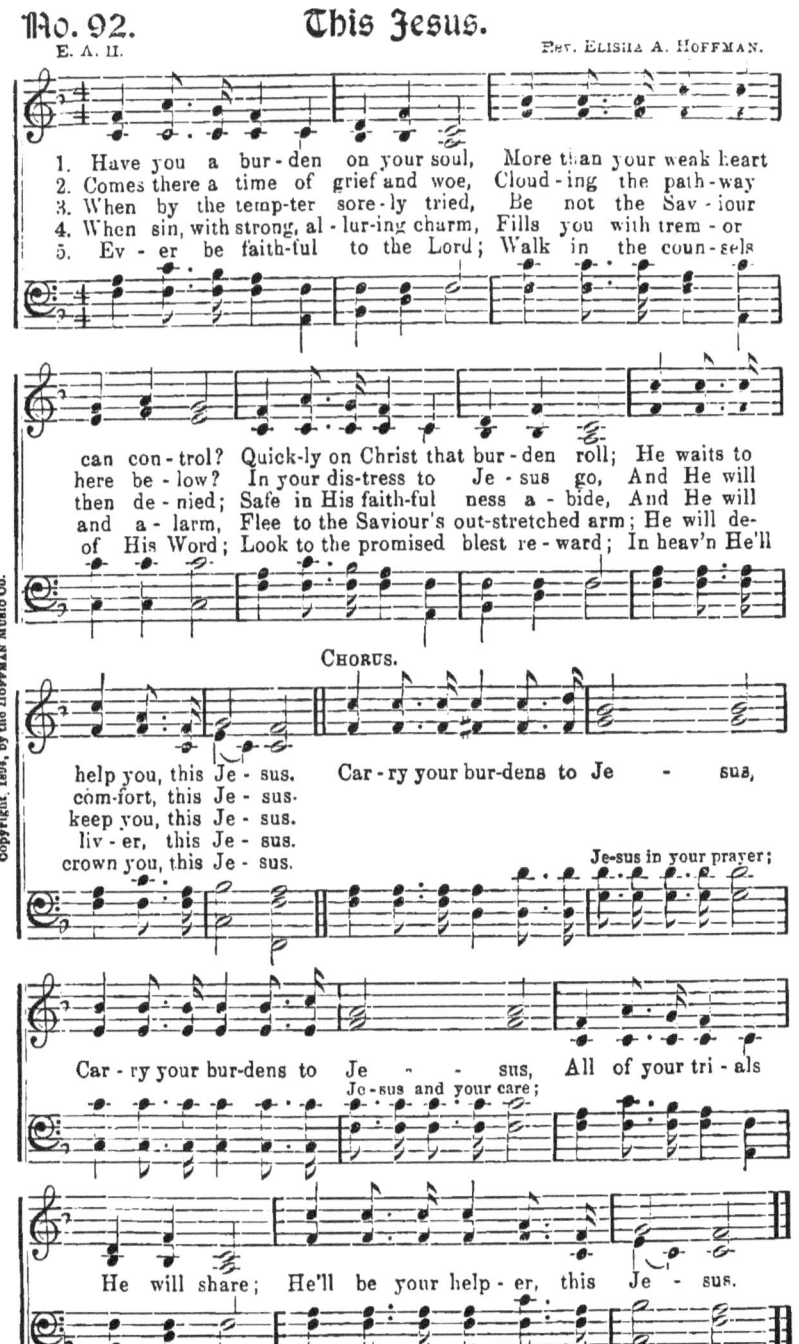

No. 94. I Am Lost.

To My Esteemed Brother and Friend, Rev. H. Beauchamp.

A dying mother, living in Polk Co., Mo., who had been for a great many years building her hopes on her strictly upright and moral character, called her children to her bedside and spoke to them in these her last words: "Dear children, I am dying now and soon must leave you all forever. I am lost, and when I leave you now I must leave you forever. You know I have always thought doing right would save me; but I know now it can not. I have made a fatal blunder and it is too late for me now, I am lost. Children, don't delay, take Christ as your Savior; lean on Him and be ready to meet your father in heaven. He is a Christian; but I am lost; and when you and your father meet in that bright world, I'll not be there. Good-bye forever."

P. M. Johnson.   C. M. Barnes.

Slow and soft, with feeling.

1. Oh, loving mothers, while you live Do not neg-lect at once to give
   Your life and heart to God's dear Son, Neglecting this, she died un-done.
2. She trod the mor-al road to death, And with her fi-nal dying breath
   Declared her sad and aw-ful fate, Re-fus-ing Christ until too late.
3. A cloud of gloom spread o'er her face, No hope in Christ without His grace,
   That moth-er sank to dark despair, Oh! mother's, pray, will you go there?

CHORUS.

Good deeds are well; but can-not save a soul from hell, or light the grave;
Your mor-al pride may sink you down Beneath a just Je-ho-vah's frown.

No. 96. **Seeking the Lost.**

P. B. Sabin.   Frank M. Davis.

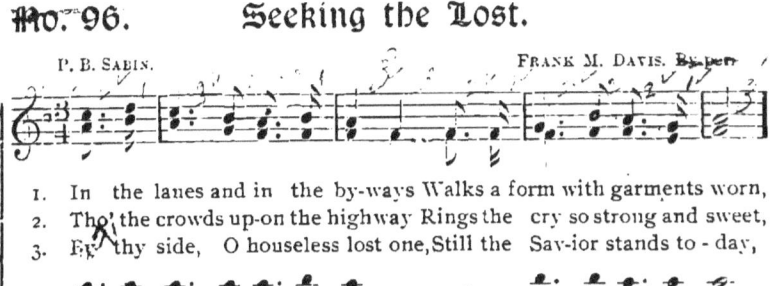

1. In the lanes and in the by-ways Walks a form with garments worn,
2. Tho' the crowds up-on the highway Rings the cry so strong and sweet,
3. By thy side, O houseless lost one, Still the Sav-ior stands to-day,

Weak and wea-ry are His foot-steps For His feet are pierc'd and torn,
Thro' the bus-y hum of traf-fic Ev-'ry ear this call doth greet,
Hear you not His ear-nest pleading, Why do you so long de-lay?

But no rest nor place He knoweth For He calls both night and day:
For the Sav-ior yearneth ev-er Souls of men to seek and save;
List, His voice so sweet and ten-der, Will you not His call o-bey?

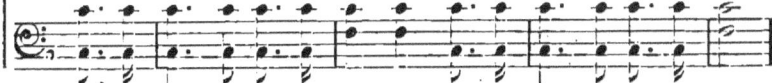

"Come, O come to love and pardon, Homeless ones that are a-stray."
'Twas for this on Calvary's mountain That His precious life He gave.
Turn to Him for love and par-don, Homeless one so far a-stray.

No. 100. Almost Persuaded.

CLIO HARPER.   T. M. CORY. Arr. C. M. B.

1. Almost hast Thou persuaded me To seek Thy shelt'ring care, (shelt'ring care)
2. Almost persuaded to be-lieve Thy blood was shed for me, (shed for me,)
3. I trembling stand on Ruin's verge, Life's seas before me roll, before me roll,

From Satan's wiles to turn and flee, The Christian's cross to bear, (cross to bear.)
And thus believing, to re-ceive Sal-va-tion full and free, (full and free.)
While strange emotions wildly surge Up-on my burden'd soul, (burden'd soul.)

CHORUS.

Al-most per-suad-ed, list ye the cry, Al-most per-suad-ed, Sav-ior, am I, Now to leave the paths of sin, And to bold-ly en-ter in The way that leads to the sky, Al-most am I.

4 The pray'rs of friends each day ascend,
   That I no more may roam,
   But now the Savior's steps attend
   To that eternal home.

5 Thy love undying let me learn,
   Nor from that love depart—
   To meekness and obed'ence turn
   This alien, stony heart.

No. 105. Sweet Home for Me.

Rev. T. J. BALLARD. C. M. BARNES, Cho. arr.

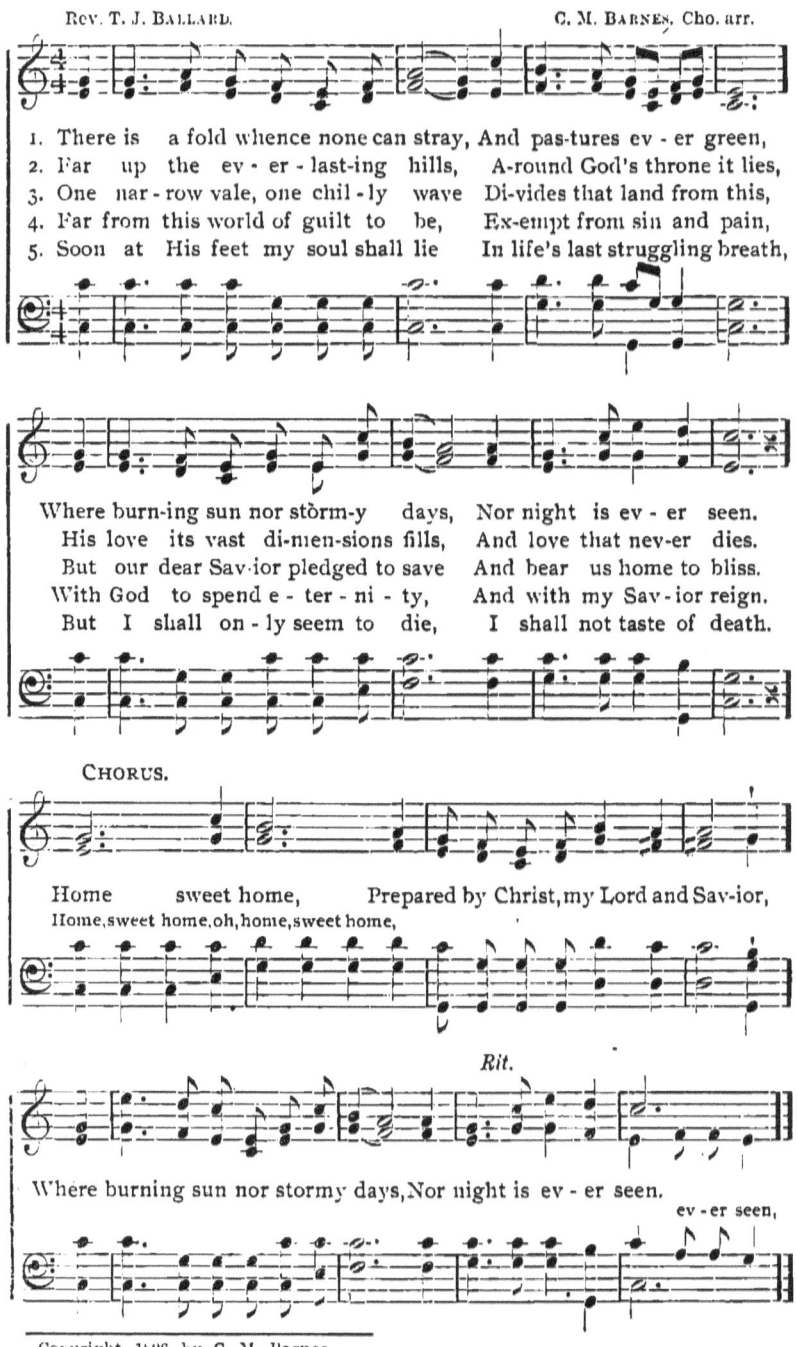

1. There is a fold whence none can stray, And pastures ev-er green,
2. Far up the ev-er-last-ing hills, A-round God's throne it lies,
3. One nar-row vale, one chil-ly wave Di-vides that land from this,
4. Far from this world of guilt to be, Ex-empt from sin and pain,
5. Soon at His feet my soul shall lie In life's last struggling breath,

Where burn-ing sun nor storm-y days, Nor night is ev-er seen.
His love its vast di-men-sions fills, And love that nev-er dies.
But our dear Sav-ior pledged to save And bear us home to bliss.
With God to spend e-ter-ni-ty, And with my Sav-ior reign.
But I shall on-ly seem to die, I shall not taste of death.

CHORUS.

Home sweet home, Prepared by Christ, my Lord and Sav-ior,
Home, sweet home, oh, home, sweet home,

Rit.

Where burning sun nor stormy days, Nor night is ev-er seen.
ev-er seen,

Copyright, 1896, by C. M. Barnes.

The World is Growing Better.—Concluded.

better ev-'ry day, Better ev-'ry day, Better ev-'ry day, The world is grow-ing bet-ter, yes, bet-ter ev-'ry day.

No. 108. Webb. 7s, 6s.

Rev. George Duffield, Jr. 1858. G. J. Webb

1. Stand up!—stand up for Je-sus! Ye sol-diers of the cross;
   Lift high His roy-al ban-ner, It must not suf-fer loss:
   From vic-tory un-to vic-tory His ar-my shall He lead,
   D. S.—Till ev-'ry foe is vanquished And Christ is Lord in-deed.

2 Stand up!—stand up for Jesus!
  Stand in His strength alone;
  The arm of flesh will fail you;—
  Ye dare not trust your own:
  Put on the gospel armor,
  And, watching unto prayer,
  Where duty calls or danger,
  Be never wanting there.

3 Stand up!—stand up for Jesus!
  The strife will not be long;
  This day the noise of battle,
  The next the victor's song:
  To him that overcometh,
  A crown of life shall be;
  He with the King of glory
  Shall reign eternally.

Every Hour I Need Thy Blessing.—Concluded.

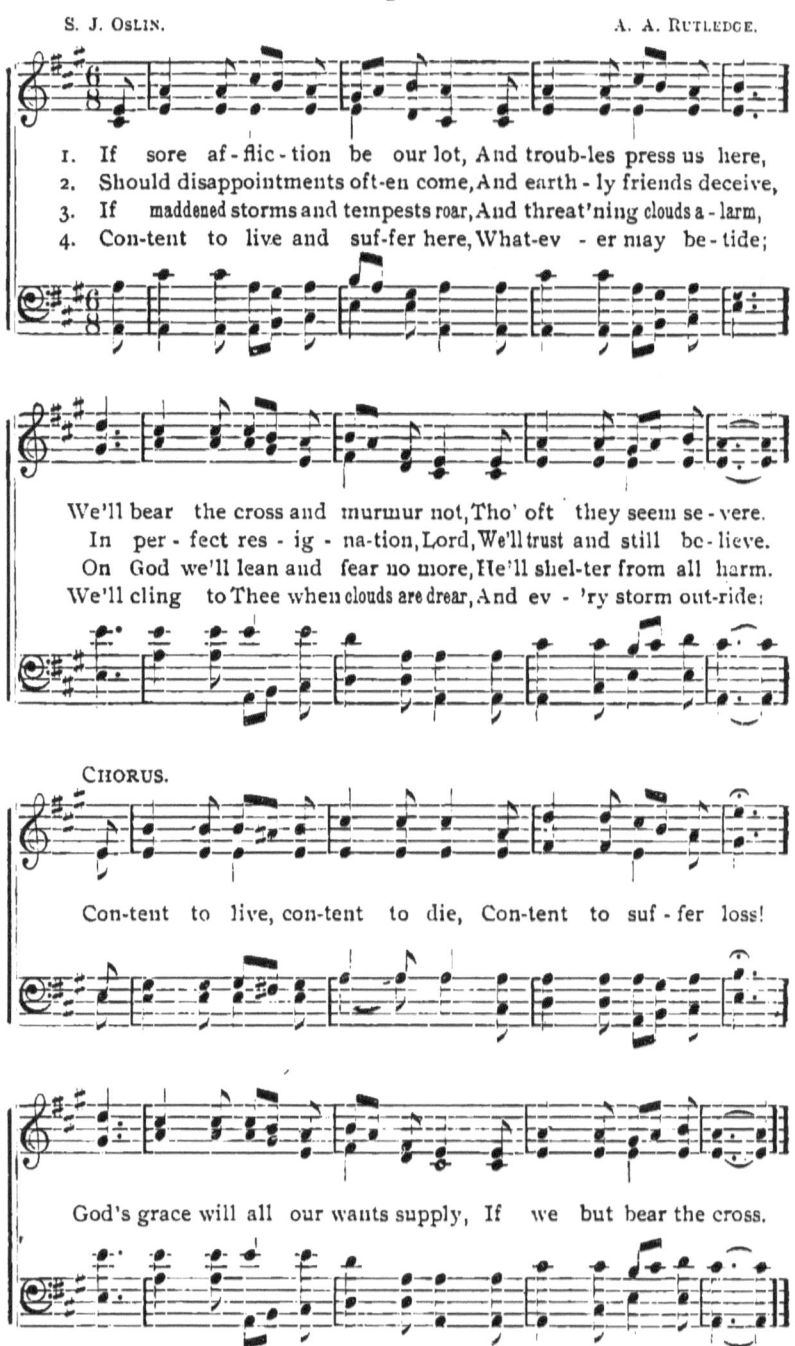

Made Perfectly Whole.—Concluded.

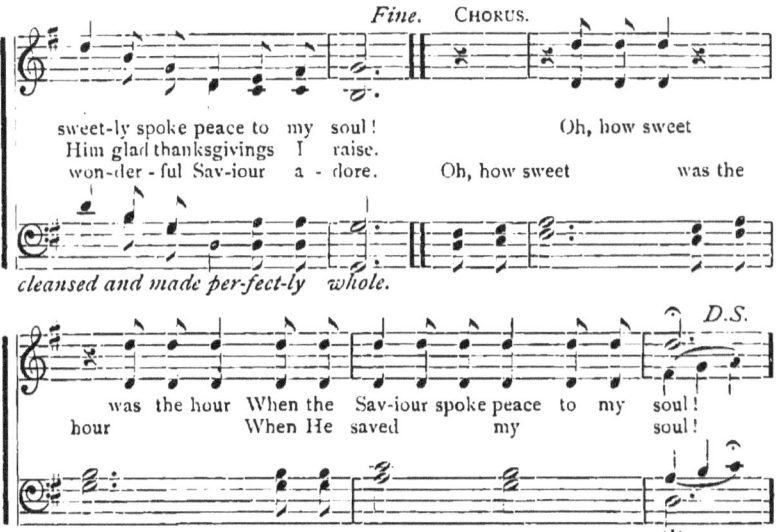

No. 123. Come Humble Sinner.

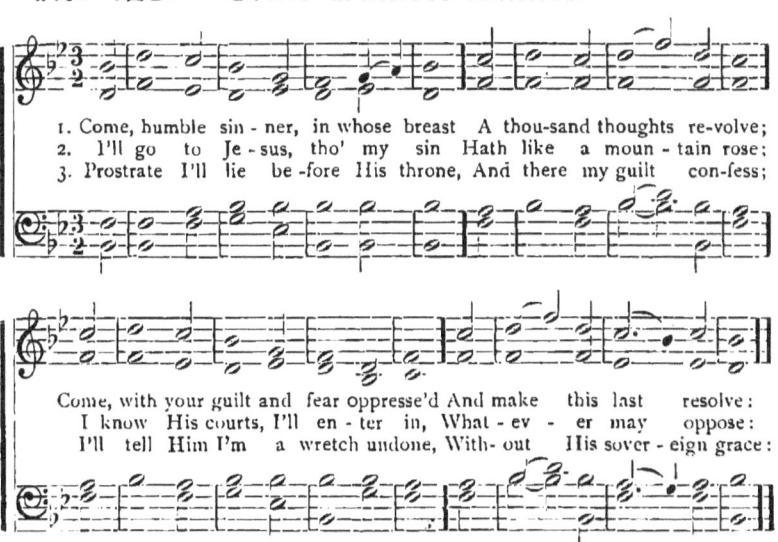

1. Come, humble sin-ner, in whose breast A thou-sand thoughts re-volve;
2. I'll go to Je-sus, tho' my sin Hath like a moun-tain rose;
3. Prostrate I'll lie be-fore His throne, And there my guilt con-fess;

Come, with your guilt and fear oppress'd And make this last resolve:
I know His courts, I'll en-ter in, What-ev-er may oppose;
I'll tell Him I'm a wretch undone, With-out His sover-eign grace:

4 I'll to the gracious King approach,
   Whose sceptre pardon gives;
   Perhaps He may command my touch,
   And then the suppliant lives.
5 Perhaps He may admit my plea,
   Perhaps will hear my prayer;
   But if I perish, I will pray,
   And perish only there.

6 I can but perish if I go,
   I am resolved to try;
   For if I stay away, I know
   I must forever die.
7 But if I die with mercy sought,
   When I the King have tried,
   This were to die (delightful thought!)
   As sinner never died.

O Why Stand Ye Idle?—Concluded.

Coda after last verse.
Slowly.

No. 127. Rock of Ages.

"The Lord is my defence, and my God is the rock of my refuge."— Psa, 94: 22.
Rev. A. M. Toplady.   Dr. Thos. Hastings.

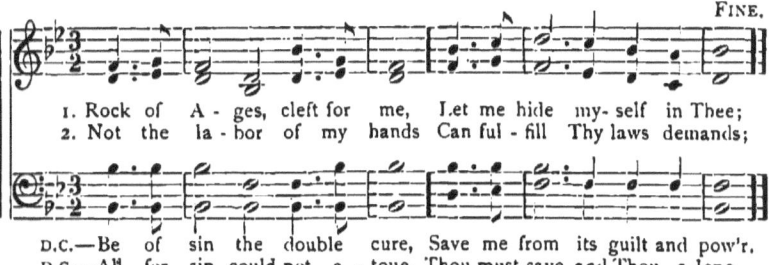

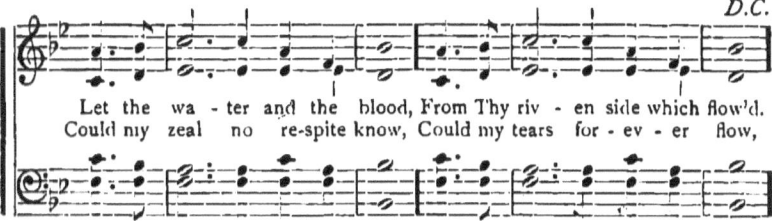

3 Nothing in my hand I bring,
  Simply to Thy cross I cling;
  Naked, come to Thee for dress,
  Helpless, look to Thee for grace;
  Foul, I to the fountain fly,
  Wash me, Saviour, or I die.

4 While I draw this fleeting breath,
  When my eyes shall close in death,
  When I soar to worlds unknown,
  See Thee on Thy judgment throne,—
  Rock of Ages, cleft for me,
  Let me hide myself in Thee.

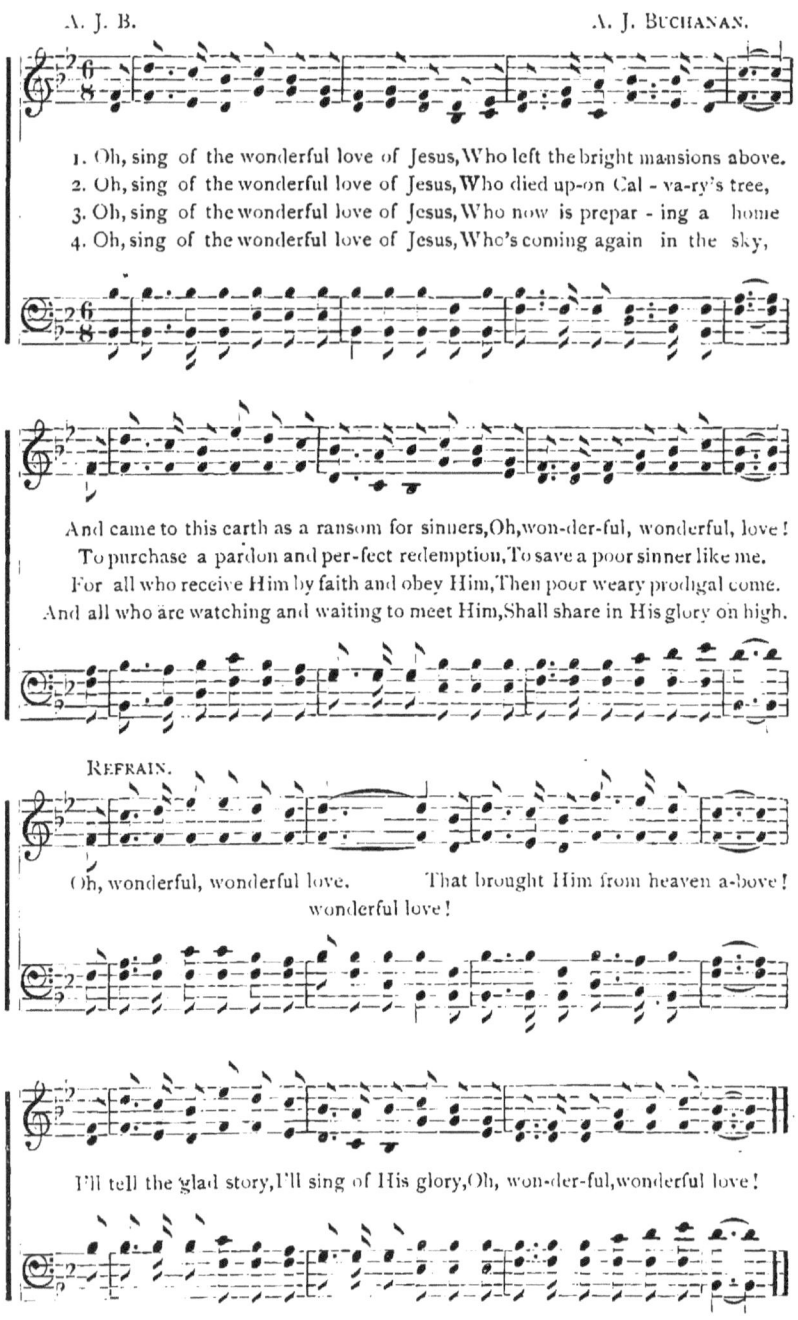

No. 130. Lead Me, Saviour.

"For Thy name's sake, lead me and guide me."—Ps. 31 : 3.

F. M. D.
Frank M. Davis. By per.

1. Sav-iour, lead me, lest I stray, . . . Gen-tly lead me all the way; . . . . . I am safe when by Thy side, ...
2. Thou the ref-uge of my soul, ... When life's stormy billows roll; . . . . . . I am safe when Thou art nigh, ... ,
3. Sav-iour, lead me, then at last, ... When the storm of life is past, ... , To the land of end-less day, ...

Sav - iour, ... lead me, lest I stray, Gen - tly . . . . lead me all the way; I . . am . . . . safe when by Thy side,

Chorus.

I would in Thy love a - bide. . . . . . . ,
All my hopes on Thee re - ly. . . . . Lead me, lead me,
Where all tears are wiped a - way. . . . . . .

I would . . . . in Thy love abide.

Sav - iour, lead me lest I stray Gen - tly down the stream of
lest I stray,

Lead Me Saviour,—Concluded.

rit - e - dim.

time (the stream of time) Lead me Sav-iour, all the way (all the way.)

No. 131. Deliverance Will Come.

"We are journeying unto a place, of which the Lord said, I will give it unto you."

J. B. M.   NUMBERS 10: 29.   REV JNO. B. MATHIAS.

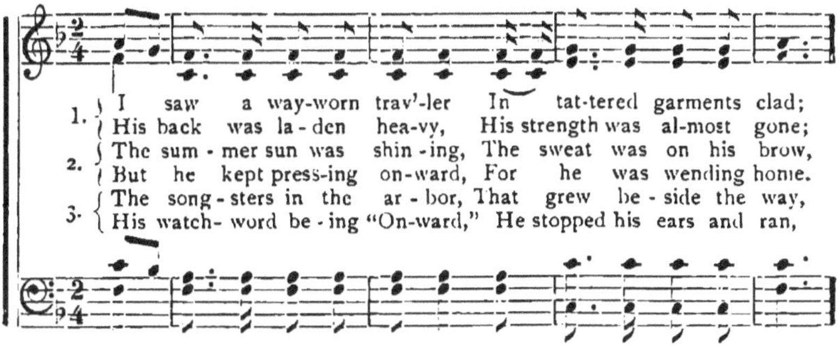

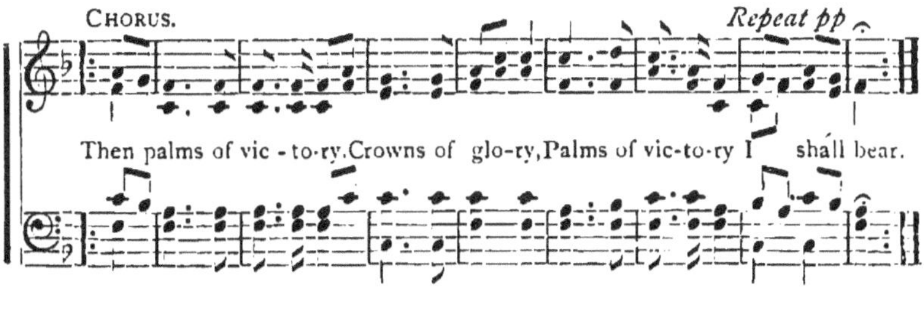

1. { I saw a way-worn trav'-ler In tat-tered garments clad;
   { His back was la-den hea-vy, His strength was al-most gone;
2. { The sum-mer sun was shin-ing, The sweat was on his brow,
   { But he kept press-ing on-ward, For he was wending home.
3. { The song-sters in the ar-bor, That grew be-side the way,
   { His watch-word be-ing "On-ward," He stopped his ears and ran,

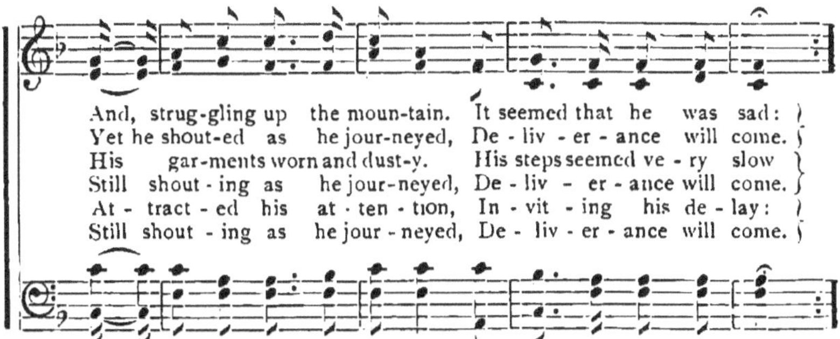

And, strug-gling up the moun-tain, It seemed that he was sad:
Yet he shout-ed as he jour-neyed, De-liv-er-ance will come.
His gar-ments worn and dust-y, His steps seemed ve-ry slow
Still shout-ing as he jour-neyed, De-liv-er-ance will come.
At-tract-ed his at-ten-tion, In-vit-ing his de-lay:
Still shout-ing as he jour-neyed, De-liv-er-ance will come.

CHORUS.   *Repeat pp*

Then palms of vic-to-ry, Crowns of glo-ry, Palms of vic-to-ry I shall bear.

INDEX.

	No. of Song.
All Alike May Come	22
Are You Washed in the Blood?	48
A Call to Praise	99
Am I a Soldier?	72
Almost Persuaded	100
Are You Shining for Jesus?	69
All, All is Free	3
Bringing in the Sheaves	103
Beautiful Stream	61
Beyond the Swelling Flood	80
Brother, Pray for My Soul	10
Bye and Bye	12
Come, Humble Sinner	123
Coming to Jesus	120
Clinging to the Rock	36
Coronation	59
Church of God, Awake!	56
Can the Lord Depend on You?	70
Crown, Harp and Song	71
Crown Him Lord of All	51
Come to Jesus Just Now	117
Death is Only a Dream	124
Deliverance Will Come	131
Don't Keep Jesus Waiting	53
Draw Me Nearer	64
Every Hour I Need Thy Blessing	112
Floating Down the Stream of Time	118
Forward, March!	37
Follow All the Way	42

	No. of Song.
God Is Coming	43
Gain After Loss	55
Greenville	81
Hear the Message	20
Hail, Thou Ever Rolling Ocean	78
Hear Our Fervent Prayer	8
How Firm a Foundation	13
I Was Glad	119
I Am The Lord's Forever	63
It Is I	46
I Would be of Use to Thee	21
I Am Resting in the Savior's Love	38
In the Shadow of the Rock	91
I Must Tell Jesus	25
I Am Coming	75
I Now Believe	87
I Am Lost	94
I've Been Washed in the Blood	6
Jesus Said It Would Be So	90
Jesus Is Calling	93
Jesus Knocks at Thy Heart	129
Kneeling, Pleading, Waiting	109
Leaning on the Everlasting Arms	132
Lead Me, Savior	130
Lead Me on	121
Love, Rest and Home	76
Lost!	24
Lay Hold on the Life-line	66
Let Us Walk in the Light	97
Light For One Step More	134

INDEX—Continued.

Title	No. of Song
Marching Onward	133
My Happy Home	47
My Precious Savior	77
My Home Above	85
Made Perfectly Whole	122
Master, Use Me	98
Martyn	5
Not Far from Heaven's Gate	1
Nettleton	57
No Dying There	26
Over the River of Light	116
Over and Over	28
Oh, the Glad, Good News	74
One More Witness for Christ	89
Over There	65
Offered to You	110
O Why Stand Ye Idle	126
Praise Ye the Lord	40
Put On the Whole Armor	101
Pity Me	27
Prepare to Meet Thy God	11
Resignation	114
Rock of Ages	127
Sweet Home for Me	105
Sweet By and By	115
Sweeping Through the Gates	2
Shall We Find Them at the Portals?	60
Say, Are You Ready?	67
Sailing On the Gospel Ship	104
Seeking the Lost	96
Save and Consecrate Me	7
Sailing O'er Life's Ocean	18
Sabbath	84
Turned Away From the Beautiful Gate	14
There's a Great Day Coming	23
Till We Meet Again	31
That Fair Land	32
Then Is the Time to Pray	41
Take a Stand for Jesus	39
The Threefold Promise	49
The Guiding Star	95
The Lost Soul's Lament	54
That Beautiful Home	52
This Jesus	92
That's Enough for Me	73
Tell It to Jesus Alone	79
Tell What The Lord Has Done	86
Tenderly Lay Her to Rest	135
The Gracious Invitation	44
There Is a Fountain	35
The World Is Growing Better	107
The Vows that I Have Taken	9
Tell It Out	4
Tell Me All About Jesus	17
The Perishing Millions	16
Where Is My Boy	82
Will I Be There?	19
Webb	108
We Shall Meet Over There	106
Walk In the Light	102
Wonderful Love	128
Work and Pray	15
Work for Jesus	62
When We All Get Home	34
Winning Precious Souls to Thee	30
What a Friend	29
Working for the Crown	55
When the Kingdom Is Come	50
When I See the Blood	88
We Praise Thee, Oh God	45
We Shall Be Satisfied	125
Whiter Than the Snow	68
Youthful Consecration	33

www.ingramcontent.com/pod-product-compliance
Lightning Source LLC
Chambersburg PA
CBHW020139170426
43199CB00010B/810